YOUR TRUE POWER

7 STEPS TOWARD DISCOVERING YOUR SOUL PURPOSE

SANDRA P. BLANES

Copyright © 2022 Sandra Pineda.

All Rights Reserved. No portion of this book may be reproduced in any form without permission from the publisher, except as permitted by U.S. copyright law.

ISBN: 978-1-951503-91-8 (Hardcover)
ISBN: 978-1-951503-85-7 (Paperback)
ISBN: 978-1-951503-86-4 (Ebook)

Authorsunite.com

CONTENTS

Introduction v

1. Embarking on Your Adventure 1
2. Finding Strength in Surrender 17
3. Connecting with Your Higher Power 25
4. Forgiving Your Dream Crushers 40
5. Rearranging Your Character 58
6. Letting Go of Heavy Stuff 71
7. Using the Space to Create 81
8. Continuing the Journey 100

Conclusion 113
About the Author 115

INTRODUCTION

> *"The greatest achievement was at first and for a time a dream. The Oak sleeps in the acorn, the bird waits in the egg, and in the highest vision of the soul, a waking angel stirs. Dreams are the seedlings of reality."*
>
> —James Allen

A dream is like a seed waiting to sprout. The seed must be planted in fertile ground, and then it needs water and sunlight. The same is true of our dreams. If our dreams are like seeds, then we must fertilize our minds in order to receive the messages they bring. How open are our minds to receiving the life deposited through our dreams? If our thoughts are the water, are we flowing with the stream of life and watering our mind? If sunlight is spirit, are we open to the sunlight of spirit for guidance, or are we consumed by ego, which blocks the light? We all have dreams and aspirations, but we're often scattering our seeds on contaminated ground. It is unlikely we will meet our maximum potential if our minds are not fertile and prepared to receive. In this book, I have gathered some simple tools that will allow you to provide the seeds of your dreams with nourishment.

You might notice an undercurrent of uneasiness as you plow through life, meeting your obligations day in and day out, until one day it becomes unbearable. Or perhaps you are feeling more than uneasy, and it is already unbearable. Our society is plagued with varying levels of depression. Our moods fluctuate between levels of feeling okay to extreme mental, emotional, physical, and/or spiritual pain. Most of us are somewhere in between. We seek professional help in a desperate attempt to regain balance. We are then given drugs to numb the pain. Yes, sometimes medication is beneficial and necessary, but many of us are overmedicated and numb.

We often turn to quick solutions like popping pills to get instant relief. Shortcuts like this have a fleeting shelf life and serious side effects. They are not solutions; they are masks. We are ignorant of the fact that many of our ailments can be solved by practicing present moment awareness. The exercises in this book, which are not religious but spiritual in nature, will help you become present and learn to live in the Now. Unfortunately, the Now is the place least visited; we are rarely present enough to even notice its existence. This is unfortunate, because the eternal present moment contains *everything* we need to live a joyful life with purpose.

Most of us live in fear of the future or regret of the past, causing ourselves pain. When the pain becomes greater than the fear of change, transformation can occur. I don't wish you pain, but there is a special kind called the *gift of desperation*. This gift, while painful, has caused many miracles. As I write these words, we are in the middle of an unprecedented global pandemic and most of us are in quarantine. There is great fear and anxiety of the unknown, but beneath the surface, there is a force rearranging our paradigm. Many lives have been lost and painful things have happened, but we've been granted a unique opportunity to take a close look at how we've been living our lives. Millions of people have been asked to suddenly stop all activity and be still. This is the first time the whole world has been called to be still at the same time.

One of the great paradoxes in life is that a calamity can cause great wisdom. The human spirit often has to be pushed to grow. It's difficult to say this, but I believe this calamity may be a gift to help humanity grow. It is here for us to face the demons within ourselves. Many of us have been running ourselves to exhaustion, working nonstop. An opportunity has been created for us to go inside ourselves and make peace with our true natures. This act of being still is causing a lot of frustration because this state has become foreign to us. After all the commotion in our lives, we are being asked to come to a screeching halt. I believe this is our chance to create a deep shift in consciousness. We now have the time to reevaluate what's truly working for us and what's not.

Collectively, we have already inflicted the same amount of pain within ourselves as this virus has in the form of greed, war, and depletion of our natural resources. This, however, is more evident because the blow has come in one fell swoop. We cannot ignore this, but herein lies the gift. We cannot wait to change because change is usually slow. We are being forced to act now. Many of us will have to reinvent ourselves. There's never been a better time to do deep work and get to the causes and conditions of why your life is not ideal. Many of us can now realize that in the pursuit of happiness. We've lost touch with the true treasures of being human, which include peace, joy, and compassion. It's time to detox. This time is a gift to be embraced. These windows of opportunity do not always come around, and we've been called to jump. Let us be wise and not return to the status quos; we must be better for it. This is the moment to prove the invincibility of our human spirit.

There is a force greater than ourselves at play. Nature can be cruel, but it's also quite clever, and for whatever reason, we are here. I urge you to seize the moment and align yourself with exterior forces that will help you—if you cooperate.

We may have profound epiphanies throughout our lives, but they are precarious. Sustaining a lasting, spiritual awakening requires resilience and willingness. These are the main ingredients needed to create the type of change in the psyche that produces lasting freedom. Throughout the lessons in this book, I will guide you through some easy-to-implement steps that will allow you to lower the volume of your ego and its incessant demands. Do not be afraid—you will not die; only the part of you that doesn't serve you will. In life, everything—both good and bad—is fighting for existence. There will be moments of inertia and fear, but the rewards will be worth it. The old system that operated your life will be replaced with new ideas that will serve you well. Keep in mind that the old will not go away without a fight—*everything* fights for survival. There will be great resistance, but you must trust the process. You deserve better than to be blackmailed by the trickery of your mind.

For many years, I was an instant-gratification junkie; there was always something missing in life. I had deep questions and wasn't getting any answers. Making bad choices to get short-term relief became a habit for me. I endured many consequences due to my ignorance, but through grace and the gift of desperation, I decided to surrender. I opened my heart to the least likely of places: divine guidance. I found that the answers I was looking for had been inside me all along, but I needed to clean up the mess to hear the guidance. Years of conditioned responses needed to be challenged. I was missing what is now obvious. It's ironic that some of life's most profound lessons are the simplest—simple lessons for complicated minds. It was hard to believe that taking a few simple steps would cause such a great shift in my life.

Life is too short to be running on systems that don't serve you. Underneath all the noise lies a still awareness that will never steer you wrong. It is silent but many times more powerful than the ego. In fact, this awareness can exist without the ego, but the ego cannot exist without it. Awareness is self-sustaining so it doesn't have to constantly reaffirm itself. This is what we must align ourselves with to find peace and our true life purpose.

Although I will lead you through exercises that can help you find peace and happiness, you must do the work. If you are like me, you will want to read the book first and then *maybe* work the exercises. You are welcome do so. However, this is a book of action; you will not get the results if you do not put in the work. I've always loved reading self-help books, but I wouldn't do the exercises. It wasn't until I put pencil to paper that I started to get results. I suggest you do the same. A new sense of discovery will emerge when you begin to write. You will discover layers within your being you didn't know were there. This is where your answers will emerge. Give yourself permission to be vulnerable.

We are three-part beings, and your body is always chiming in. You will be surprised at how your entire being will cooperate when you are feeling inspired. All your parts will be working in synchrony. This all begins by being true to yourself. Communicate to every part of yourself that you are about to embark on a magical journey, a journey of healing and discovery. Allow all parts of your being to become congruent. There may be resistance, but allow for this, too. It is natural for resistance to emerge because the old systems will fight for their survival. Many of these systems come from a place of survival, so in a sense they are trying to serve us. But now we wish to move beyond survival and into higher states.

Nature abhors vacuums, and spaces are always being filled. Change is uncomfortable and those old little devils (your habits or tendencies) will kick and scream, but soon they will be replaced and relief will come. Do not remove an old system without replacing it with a new one, or you run the risk of someone else or something else filling it for you. In all your affairs, follow your heart. Listen and choose that which rings true. Becoming still in present awareness is the goal. This is the place where the answers to your unfulfilled dreams lie. Therein lies the peace that surpasses all understanding. Once you have tasted it, it won't be long before you break the strongholds of your mind and shed your false identity.

The answers to all your questions lie within. Life can be a joyful experience because we all come from a place of love deep inside. We are infinite beings living inside confined structures that provide stability for our material existence. By following the spiritual principles in this book, you will realize your true nature, which is benign, joyous, and free. The twelve spiritual principles you will be practicing are:

1. Honesty
2. Hope
3. Surrender
4. Courage
5. Integrity
6. Willingness
7. Humility
8. Love
9. Responsibility
10. Discipline
11. Awareness
12. Service

This book guides you through several exercises centered on these spiritual principles that will lead you to liberation. As you work through them, you will find that what lies beneath your behaviors are all layers of preconditioned responses. Each of us must do the best we can within this lifetime to be free. Grant yourself this auspicious opportunity for true growth. The fact you are reading these words and are willing to try means your transformation has begun. Congratulations!

At first glance, these exercises will not make sense. This is because they are spiritual in nature rather than logical. We must bypass the logical mind. The exercises may seem too easy or irrelevant. This is because we are trying to connect our hearts to our minds. We are trained to work in reverse, and to the mind, it will not make sense. Please follow these exercises in order so they will be clearer to you. If this does not work for you, once you are done, you can always go back to your old self. It won't be far, but if you are brave and willing to give this a wholehearted shot, it *will* work for you. Your willingness to want more will summon all the forces in the universe, and they will come to your aid. This book is one of those forces. It has arrived in your hands because you've summoned it on some level. You have helped me create it. Thank you!

I share these exercises with you because they changed my life. Similar versions of these exercises are used across the world for a cascade of issues. I've condensed them, but these are the steps and principles found in most 12-step programs. The same principles are used time and again to help people overcome helpless states. Following these steps and discovering their principles literally saved my life. Of course, I had to follow the instructions and put in the work. The changes did not happen overnight, but soon my family and friends began to notice a shift in me (people around us will usually notice our change in attitudes before we do). My sister Elizabeth was so impressed by the results she noticed in me that she wondered why these steps were not more readily accessible to everyone. She believed everyone could use these exercises, not just people caught in extreme destructive patterns.

As time passed and I began to see the major changes within myself, I became more empathetic and started noticing the suffering of those around me. The truth is that most of us are suffering in one form or another. We mostly struggle with some form of persistent emotional distress. People who I'd thought had it all together began to show traces of uneasiness and pain. I soon realized it's not just people with extreme obsessive disorders who were living in pain. As I analyzed what the connecting thread of this pain could be, I realized it was the misuse of our minds. Our incessant negative and anxiety-filled thoughts were the main causes of our woes. It was an epiphany for me. I remembered my wise sister's comments, and I was inspired to write this book.

Working the exercises in this book will give you the clarity to go beyond your ego (the major cause of woes) and into your true self. Your higher self has been silently waiting to be discovered your whole life. I do not claim that, once you've read this book and worked the exercises, you will instantaneously have all the answers you seek. I do, however, claim you will be transformed in a way that allows space for freedom and creativity to flow. You will be free of old thought patterns that no longer serve you. Fears and resentments will lose their grip and your life will have new meaning.

I believe we are all connected, and your spirit helped to inspire this creation. I am humbled and grateful that you are ready to embark on this journey. My wish is that, out of your pain and dissatisfaction with life, you will find the joy and freedom that is your birthright. Congratulations on not settling on a life half lived. There will be moments when some of the steps may not make sense, but trust the process. You are here because your higher self has led you. The impulse of creation will always aid the seeking soul. I am with you in spirit and in love.

1
EMBARKING ON YOUR ADVENTURE

"It's never too late to be what you might have been."

—George Eliot

Have you derailed from following your dreams? Have you lost all traces of childlike qualities that used to fill your eyes with wonder? While most of us are functioning as members of society, it should not come at the price of compromising our dreams. I understand that complacent feeling all too well. Due to my unhappiness and the inability to deal with life, I became self-destructive.

Despite being an outgoing and hard-working person, at age thirty I woke up in a very dark place. I realized I'd live most of my life in nonstop action. I had my first child at eighteen, my first business at twenty-three, and my second business at twenty-seven. There were moments when I'd briefly realize I was in a constant coverup from my true self. To keep those feelings at bay, I'd stay busy. The busier I was, the less I had to remember any distant, painful memories. The day came when my inner self stepped up, and I was forced to take a real look at my life. Despite all my accomplishments, I had a deep feeling of disconnection. I became extremely materialistic and superficial. I felt like an imposter, and my incessant stream of negative thoughts would not stop. I was deeply unsatisfied with my life and unhappy with my work. I began to isolate and fell into a deep depression. I went to psychologists and psychiatrists, but nothing helped for long. Then I became fixated on the idea that the right romantic relationship would be the answer, which made me needy and insecure. When that didn't work, I turned to chemical substances, including pills and alcohol, and that sure didn't work.

My negativity increased. I became a pessimist and began to lose hope in humanity. I could not help but see all the wrong and injustice in the world. It became unbearable, and I was at a crossroads. It's always darkest before the dawn. There are times when we've gone so far down the scale that there is no other place but up, and this is what happened to me. Out of my despair, I became humble. Once I became humble, I was able to see a glimpse of hope. Finally, I became willing to be teachable. I was introduced to these beautiful spiritual principles, and then joy flourished in my life once again.

WHY HAVE YOU ABANDONED YOUR DREAMS?

There are many excuses for abandoning our dreams. We might have been born into unfortunate circumstances or might have simply chosen to fulfill someone else's expectations. The bottom line is, we are left leading an unfulfilled life that takes tremendous amounts of energy to navigate. Look inside and see if you are feeling tired and unmotivated or become easily bored; those feeling might have become so familiar that they seem normal. They are not. Not one of us should settle for a less than a fulfilling life. I'm not saying life will always be easy.

I am saying the good days should far outnumber the bad days. When we are unfulfilled, there is an internal battle happening. Part of us cannot deny this void, while the other side is trying to "protect" us by reminding us things are not so bad.

These are the roles society has taught us, but there is major incongruence. We use up all the energy we can muster to keep those systems in place. Why? Because we are creatures of habit, and anything that involves a little effort and courage is better left alone. However, there comes a point when the pain of remaining as we are is greater than the fear of change, and we come to a crossroad. At that point, many of choose to anesthetize with drugs and alcohol or overwork, and then come home and zone out in front of the television. Seeking an outlet is not bad in itself, but this is not where our true freedom lies.

Many of us may come to a point of suffering where we give up, and there is more than one way to do it. Some will simply settle for what life has handed them, feeling an occasional undercurrent of misery. There are those who dive into drugs or alcohol to obtain temporary relief, and then there are those who choose to check out. Have you ever wondered what the cause of all this misery could be? I did. Day in and day out, I pounded my head with the question: *Why? What the heck is wrong with me?* The truth is, it wasn't just me; it is many of us. Don't be fooled by people who seem to have it together on the outside; on the inside, they may be carrying great loads of pain and unfilled dreams. I congratulate you and thank you for trusting this journey into freedom. You are a seeker, and you shall find the freedom and joy you are looking for.

THE SPIRITUAL PRINCIPLES BEHIND THE EXERCISES

At first, the exercises may not seem relevant to your problems, but I have come to discover that in life, there are a few good solutions to almost all problems, regardless of their nature. Certain spiritual principles are universal, and when we live by them, we are in accord with the universe. Suddenly walls become doors serving as portals to new realities. We must live by these principles if we are to be free from the bondage of ego. In the end, you will likely find that most of your problems are of your own making; it is a beautiful truth, for it allows you the power to change. If you are reading these words, you are a person of courage. This is not for the weak. Not everyone is ready to trade in their life situation for a better one. If these words ring with truth, your spirit will let you know.

Please remember that these are spiritual instructions, and they will never make sense to your logical mind. For the time being, I ask you to set aside any prejudice and have faith in the process. It has worked for thousands of people and can work for you. The measure of success will depend on your surrender and sense of urgency to work through these divinely inspired exercises. Don't wait to hit rock bottom for a sense of urgency to take these actions. There is a greater need for this guidance than ever before in history. The amount of torture caused by our minds and the stress in our lives has become an epidemic. This type of work is not for people who need it; it's for those want it. You must be willing to put in the work necessary for true liberation. Then you will be in a position to share this knowledge with others, for we are all looking for freedom.

BRING YOUR WILLINGNESS TO DREAM

Throughout our lifetime, toxicity accumulates within our minds and lodges itself as a part of our personalities. It is not easy to undo the mess created over years. As I have mentioned, the pain has to be greater than the fear of change. This is no quick fix, but it won't take nearly as long as it took to create the mess. The universe tends to lean toward simple solutions; once we start exercising them, a domino effect will take place. Before you know it, positive changes will occur.

There will always be trends and quick fixes. What we need are lasting and life-fulfilling solutions. I have practiced the "Law of Attraction," and I believe it can work; However, you probably won't attract something that is not already yours in consciousness—especially if you feel you don't deserve it. When you are in a good place, you will attract good things. But the trick is getting to that good place. You can't fool creation. You can visualize all you want, but if you aren't truly feeling it, you will not get the result. Eventually, you will get tired of trying, give up, and think it did not work. Many of these methods work, but you have to condition yourself to be in the right place first.

There is one quality you are asked to bring to the table: willingness. This is a gift you must give yourself; in fact, it is the grandest gift you can give. No one can give it to you, no matter how much they love you. I will share principles with you that work, I will give you the sequence to follow, and I will share ideas and concepts I have discovered along the way. But *you* must bring your willingness. I know these ideas and concepts will ring true with your inner self and you will be prompted into action. The practice of these spiritual principles will begin to clear the baggage of your past and make room for the life you are meant to live. I will serve as your guide, but the answers will come from within you.

Learning to be present is key on your quest to discovering true joy and finding your life purpose. Being present is the main ingredient for developing a fertile mind from which the seeds of your dreams can sprout. There is fertile ground deep within each of us, as well as a dream we never birthed. I was able to realize my dream and so can you. I know this truth because life does not take sides.

Many of us have built systems to support our egos, and they won't go easily. If we begin to shed layers at a time, finding our life purpose becomes easier. This journey of exploration will teach you how to harness a fertile mind built for lasting happiness.

Happiness is at the center of our soul. I am referring to our soul as the eternal part of us that connects us to our source. I believe too many of us have lost the joy of living, which is something that should come naturally. Many of us are out of balance with our true nature. We are not machines; we are intelligent beings that are spiritual in nature and constantly evolving. We are evolving with the impulse of creation and seven billion years of experience backing us. We are not running the show, nor do we have to do this alone. We must wake up to the beauty we are. We must love fiercely and remember to dream once more.

Dreams are all around us; at some point everything was composed this way. For anything to have come into existence, it must have been dreamed. I believe dreams and imagination are closely related; however, when I use the word *dream*, I mean *imagination infused with desire*. The final ingredient needed to materialize this nebulous intent is belief. Everyone dreams; dreams come from a very profound place within your being. I like the word *dream* because to me it sounds like an unborn reality waiting to be birthed. Your ultimate life purpose is to be alive, but while you are here, you might as well follow your heart's call. Time is still going to pass you by whether you are happy or sad. Why not enter the timelessness? Life is truly beautiful, but you must have the eyes to see and dare to dream once more. Dreams are ignited in our hearts.

Unfortunately, we are not taught to trust our inner guidance signals. Many of us have been downplaying our life's experiences and lying to each other. In an attempt to co-sign each other's "downplaying" attempts, we've contaminated our fertile ground with our fears. As children, we really had no choice in the matter; our minds were pure. Little by little, we were told certain things; we were belittled or ridiculed. We were told our dreams were nonsense and we should be realistic. However, there is nothing more realistic than a dream. As a child, you may have wanted to be an actor, a singer, or an astronaut. Children don't compromise their dreams, wondering which career would pay them more handsomely. They don't think they are being unrealistic; they dare to dream.

Over the millennia, ancient wisdom has guided us to be childlike in our approach to life in order to experience the wonder and beauty all around us. This ability is never lost, only covered up. It lives deep within us, reminding us how unhappy we are when we are not doing what we love. The obvious secret is that all of this is happening right here and now, right before our very eyes. We must learn to look through the eyes of the heart, which exists in the present moment. We are seldom present enough to rejoice in the magnificence of the Now, and the most obvious space is hidden in plain sight. We've been blinded. Inside, each of us senses there is something great we are missing. If you will learn to dream and have an open mind, marvelous things will happen. Just as you had to learn to be unhappy and settle for your lot in life, you can learn to regain your innate state of joy.

We are all on a search for life, liberty, and happiness. In the end, each of us is looking for happiness and freedom in our own way. Raising our level of consciousness will always bring a sense of freedom. This, in turn, brings more love and connectivity toward nature and others. The byproduct is the joy of existence. Once you find this joy, everything will fall into place because it is joy you seek. Remember, I'm not talking about a fleeting thrill. I'm talking about the joy of living, which comes from higher self-awareness, freedom, and love. Once you have attained this state, it won't matter where you are. Your whole life will become your altar. You will welcome your life's unfolding, and any situation you are in will become better. You will not be a hostage to the illusion of the five senses. You will transcend them and find greater meaning and purpose in your life. These realities exist as constants inside all of us since the day we were born. We once felt this as children, but somewhere along our lives, we chose to forget.

I still retain the memories of "once upon a time" when it was still clear in mind. I also recall making the choice to forget. When I was about four or five years old, I remember having a profound knowing of where we came from and why we were here. I remember this deep understanding. I can compare it to a perfect symphony of knowingness in my heart. I recall watching the adults act as if they'd forgotten something. They seemed to be in a play. Slowly, it became clear I was to forget, too. I don't remember exactly why, but I do know it was quite clear I must forget. I suspect the reason for forgetting was to experience this aspect of reality and later return to higher consciousness, more freedom, and a greater capacity to love. It is all divinely intended. We cannot fail, but we can choose to be active participants in the unfolding.

ELIMINATE INCESSANT THINKING

One of our biggest struggles in discovering our life purpose is incessant thinking. I'm not talking about creative, useful thoughts. I'm referring to our tormentors, the ones that steal so many precious hours of our days. This incessant thinking has become an epidemic, and it is the main cause of our woes. It robs us from the present moment where miracles and discoveries take place. All our answers are found in the present moment, but we must learn to stay there. Incessant thoughts are the reason many turn to drugs, alcohol, and other harmful coping mechanisms. For some, it gets so bad they even choose to end their lives.

It is a paradox that one of our most wonderful and creative tools can work against us. The mind is powerful, but many of us don't know how to use it. We must learn to connect our hearts with our minds; otherwise, we are destined to be bullied by our minds for life. We are complex beings with matrix upon matrix of thought patterns and responses compiled over years. We train ourselves to make use of these habitual forms of thinking and start to believe that we *are* our thoughts and mental processes.

We are not our thoughts; we are points of consciousness, spiritual in nature, who have been granted this wonderful ability to analyze and keep or discard different experiences. What was meant as a gift has become a liability. This can be reversed. It takes the same amount of energy to entertain a negative thought as it does a positive one, yet the effects for the negative are far less beneficial. A thought is a form of intelligent energy that emits frequencies. Many of life's great masters tell us the world in which we live was created by thoughts. Collectively, all our thoughts are contributing to the whole. Just imagine the power of our thoughts in our personal reality.

Throughout the day, we have random thoughts. We automatically create a succession of thoughts that may leave us depressed or confused. Since many of these thoughts are random and incoherent, we push them down and try to refocus on the task at hand. The act of pushing them down gives us the false sense we've stripped them of their power. We believe they can just vanish. The truth is they will not. All thoughts have a life span. They'll leave residue that interacts with your current thoughts and experiences. Oftentimes, they are the guiding forces behind our current circumstances without our awareness.

One of my favorite quotes by Carl Jung reads, "Until you make the unconscious conscious, it will direct your life and you will call it fate." If we're to take charge of our destinies, we must awaken to this truth. All thoughts we believe in have power. There are many thoughts and memories that we honor with great belief that are simply not true. Others may have been true in the past but are no longer serving us. While the power to change is within us, we must all be guided to higher and higher levels of truth and become more conscious beings.

The fact you are the generating force behind your thoughts means you have control over their influence on you. Memories will always crop up, but this does not mean they should take you hostage. When you are triggered by an emotional thought, it creates an imprint in your mind. It then creates a negative expression, installed as a tool that will not suit your evolution into higher consciousness, unless it is used intelligently. We all do this hundreds of times a day. Unless we learn how to turn the negative expression into a lesson, we are not only losing the precious energy needed to create, but we are also making ourselves sick. Incessant thinking creates unnecessary suffering. We are seemingly powerless to calm the storm of thoughts attacking us throughout the day, coming in the form of worst-case scenarios and filling us with anxiety and depression.

Many of us are consumed by what others think of us. One reason many of us are so concerned about what others think of us is because we are judgmental and critical ourselves. We try to quiet the tormentor in our heads by noticing the wrong in others to feel better about ourselves. We've come up with all kinds of distorted conclusions to keep our own thoughts at bay. Once we learn how to still our minds, we will begin to have more compassion toward ourselves. Love thrives in silence. This kind of silence creates introspection instead of criticism. When we learn to be kinder to ourselves, we will not find the need to be so critical of others. Once we are filled with empathy and compassion, the fear of facing ourselves will dissipate.

Incessant negative thinking can make our lives feel unmanageable as it drains us of the energy needed to perform our daily tasks. Sometimes they are subtle, other times evident. Many times, our thoughts cause us to lash out at others and ruin relationships. The sad thing is how many people are just going through life as if this is completely normal. Just because many are participating does not make it natural. If you are not feeling fulfilled in life and you know something is wrong, you have been alerted by the infinite intelligence within you that something is not right. Be brave and do not settle when there is so much more to discover within yourself. There will always be ups and downs in life, but your good days should greatly outnumber the bad. Sadly, there are people who can't even remember the last time they had a good day. You do not have to be one of them.

Some people are afraid to feel good because they are always waiting for the other shoe to drop. It is the mind's biggest deception that security lies in doubt and protection lies in fear. Our sense of doubt and fear can serve us if we are in imminent physical danger, but they should not become a constant pattern of protection. We are so accustomed to this state that we've granted our minds permission to keep us safe in the realm of this known misery. It becomes incredibly difficult to express any type of creative expansion because fear will frustrate our efforts every time. We must take a leap of faith because growth will feel like pain.

Don't confuse pain with danger. It is only the impulse of creation breaking through. If you are lucky, there will come a moment when the pain is greater than the fear of change, and change will be summoned. When this happens, you must be willing to take a hard look at your recurring thoughts and see them for what they are: ghosts from your past. The life they hold is just a memory you have made into a part of yourself. The memory or the action may have happened, but it only lives in your mind. Thoughts from your past carry residual energy in the form of a memory. These memories interact with your current thoughts and create conclusions that are incongruent and out of touch with reality. You then form erroneous conclusions and take unhelpful actions. When this happens, you are not creating from your current reality; you are reacting from past imprints in your mind and your perceptions and decisions are jaded.

Thoughts and memories are triggered very quickly, and although we may not have control over their speed and randomness, we can become aware of them, thereby creating enough presence to become self-aware. You will then not be taken hostage as easily by unconscious tendencies. Emotionally charged memories have a strong hold on us. There is no use getting into a street fight with our minds. There is a gentler way to create the psychic change needed for lasting happiness and freedom. We must adapt new tools and continue to replace old patterns with new ones.

There is another memory-saving mechanism we possess. Eckhart Tolle, in his book *The Power of Now*, calls it the pain body. He explains how the emotional pain we experience leaves behind a residue of pain that lives within us. Current pain then becomes entangled to pain from our past and can go all the way back to our childhood. We then carry this pain (usually emotional) within our bodies, and each time we become unconscious and it is triggered, it arises. This pain body may be triggered suddenly by a thought or memory from our past, and we run the risk of spilling our reactive behavior into our current interactions unnecessarily. This happens very quickly, usually before we are aware it is happening. Tolle goes on to say it's as if this pain body creates an entity of its own. As automatic a response as this may seem, we can be free of this type of reactive behavior by becoming present and aware of our current states. By becoming present enough, we can observe the trend, rather than being hijacked by our thoughts.

A Power Greater Than Ourselves

We are powerful creators, but most of us are creating by default. Once we are free from the stagnant energy of our past, we will see how easily one thought can replace another. We will be given the freedom to choose our thoughts. One thought at a time, we change our destinies.

A choice is only a choice if we believe we have one. Because our thoughts seem so random and automatic, it is difficult to see how we do have a choice in what we think. There is hardly any space between thoughts to create the possibility of choosing a new one, and we are basically hostages to our thoughts. When we are up against such a fight, the power of choice is weak. We need to find a power greater than ourselves to regain our sanity. Insanity is doing the same things over and over and expecting different results. The gift of choice is many times more powerful when we align it with a power greater than ourselves.

To reboot our biological computer and become effective at changing our thought patterns, we must first undertake an internal housecleaning. This can be accomplished by doing the exercises in this book. Many times, our decisions reflect our fears instead of our hopes because we store negative memories from our past. Our default mode must be courage. One of the exercises in this book will ask you to align yourself with a power greater than yourself. You will need it to conquer your incessant thinking and help you on your journey through self-discovery. You are free to find any power you choose. It doesn't have to be religion, but it can be. If you already have one, great! This will be a wonderful opportunity to bond with this power. If you do not have a higher power, I will guide you toward finding your own in Chapter 3.

The point is, we must align ourselves with forces of courage and summon faith. We must replace fear and doubt. The only way to replace fear and doubt is with courage and hope. You will find a benign power, one that is on your side. The exercises in this book call you to surrender to divine guidance; life will take on new meaning when you are under the direction and care of a loving higher power. Your human power got you this far. You will now need to find a power greater than yourself. Once you taste this type of freedom, you will realize no external event can ever affect you without your consent.

There was a very dark time in my life when I was a victim to the whims of circumstance. My most creative solution was to drink to forget. I drank because of my mom, global warming, human cruelty, relationships, work, and my cat. There was always a good reason. There really was no use trying because life was going to hell. In time, I realized I was the jailer, and my mind was my prison. I reached a breaking point. Luckily, I made it out alive; some are not so lucky. There comes a moment when we are in enough pain to either self-destruct or reconstruct. The good thing about pain is how we can only take so much before we take action—or it takes us. The road to reconstruction is scary but fascinating.

Make Your Choice

There are many adventures on the horizon. There are times when you will not see a horizon, but every sailor knows that to discover new worlds, one must lose sight of land for some time. The mess that has taken years to create can quickly be restored to order by earnestly working these spiritual principles.

Most of us move robotically through our days and are not aware we are making choices all the time. Not choosing is still a choice. If you do not choose, it will be chosen for you, but not always to your advantage. The decisions we make are many times subconscious agreements from long ago. The good ones serve us well, but the negative ones need replacing. All action is born in thought, no matter how automatically it arises. Many times, these impulses feel more like automatic reflexes than thoughts. These reflexes are thoughts impressed upon us long ago by people or life events. We must learn to identify our thoughts to better control and direct them. It is very difficult to take control of a thought when it is emotionally charged, but there is a way. This process I will share with you is tried and true. You can always keep what works for you and change what doesn't. These are simply a set of instructions meant for attaining true freedom.

We think we are free, but we are prisoners of our minds. Once you are free, you can then create from a place of hope instead of fear. We all struggle in life. Pain is mandatory, but suffering is optional. Grief is a natural healing process, but when it is extended into a lifetime of suffering, it is defeating its purpose. It may not be so obvious, but a constant undercurrent of sadness should not be acceptable. Slowly this undercurrent will creep into to your relationships, your work, and your health. Many useful tools will turn against us when we use them as ends instead of means.

We must learn to work through our problems in a new light. When we are confronted with a situation, we are allowed a certain amount of time to process it before it gets lodged into our subconscious, and then we will have to fish for it. We must get uncomfortable and trust in the process to follow what makes sense in our hearts. We must learn to deal with our problems, not stuff them away and pretend they will vanish, because they will not. Our feelings are forms of energy that cannot be created or destroyed, but they can be transformed. If we had been taught these lessons as children, we would have better learned how to work through our problems.

It is better late than never, and now is your time. Thankfully, many people have crossed the road before you and are willing to help. You must commit to the process that best resonates with you. Again, there are many paths, but only one destination. Freedom creates joy, peace, and all the fruits of the spirit. These are the true ingredients the world needs most. If we learn to translate from a place of love, we will realize how behind every negative thought is a demand trying to be filled in sometimes elegant disguises. We will see them as the pouts of an angry child who didn't get their way. We will realize we are not our thoughts and there is a loving intelligence behind each one. It is important to learn to recognize this and embrace it instead of condemning and punishing ourselves.

We should learn to look beyond the obvious and coax our little devils, for we are not our thoughts. As real as they may seem, they are only messengers seeking expression through the outlet of our minds. Please don't shoot the messenger, and don't shoot yourself. In sparing the lives of our thoughts, instead of pushing them down, and acknowledging them we begin to understand ourselves at deeper levels. Practice this in the spirit of love. There is no memory, no thought or event within your mind that would kill you, even though it feels like it. It's only the anticipation of the thought that creates such agony.

2
FINDING STRENGTH IN SURRENDER

Spiritual Principle: Honesty

"This above all: to thine own self be true, And it must follow, as the night the day, Thou canst not then be false to any man."

—William Shakespeare

The word *surrender* is often attributed to weakness. However, within this concept lies great strength. The spiritual principle behind the exercise in this chapter is honesty. Before we can actualize any change, we must become honest and admit something in our life is not working for us. While we are still in the grips of trying to do it ourselves, there is no room for surrender.

Once we surrender and admit our way is not working, we can then begin the reconstruction process. We must surrender our old ways and have faith that there is a better way. We have all acquired a set of tools to help us navigate through life. Some of these tools may be in the form of excuses and resentments to justify our behaviors. For the most part, we are blind to these automatic responses. More often, we will only see their consequences. It is not easy to admit this; your ego will blind you, but it's true. Even though we all have different struggles, they are simply different versions of the same ones. The most common is our incessant negative thinking, which brings with it all types of fear.

AWARENESS OF YOUR INCESSANT THINKING MIND

Awareness is the first step within the process of reconstruction with any major ailment. I will use incessant thinking because I believe it is the major cause of humanity's afflictions. *You must reach the point where you become aware of your incessant thinking and that your life situation is not working for you.*

The strength in surrender is how it can be used for any struggle. We must become aware in order to change because doing so makes us humble and teachable. One cannot initiate true change while the ego is inflated. It is not easy to admit defeat over something as insidious as incessant thinking. Our mind might tell us it's not a problem. It will tell us it's normal and remind us how everyone is doing it. It will take a great amount of courage to surrender, but it is necessary to find freedom.

It will always get darker before it gets light, but don't give up. Incessant thinking has become a form of dysfunction leading to many forms of mental illness. There are times when it's necessary to visit a professional and get adequate help. If this is essential for you, professional help will get you to the place where it will be easier for you to work on yourself. Just make sure you are not overmedicating yourself as a form of a bandage instead of dealing with your real issues. Still, there comes a time when no human power will be able to help. There may be guides and therapists, but the true transformation must come from within. It is a fact that pain is a great motivator. However, you do not always have to be in a desperate position to better yourself. Perhaps you are aware of what's happening and just need a gentle reminder that some action is needed.

As I mentioned, you may not be inclined toward working these exercises. That's fine too. The information I am sharing will benefit everyone. Once you are aware of the dysfunction, it will no longer have as much power over you. It will create a space, but as with everything in life, you get out what you put in. It comes with the cosmic law of causation, or cause and effect. You don't have to wait to become dysfunctional to become better.

It will serve our children and all of humanity once we learn to align our mind with our heart's energy. Trust that there is a power greater than yourself guiding you every step of the way. Its innate intelligence regulates the beats of your heart, your breathing, and all your basic functions. It operates from your subconscious mind and is millions of times more intelligent than the conscious mind. I'm not trying to strip you of your treasures. The mind is a wonderful thing. I am always awestruck by analytical people when they use their intellect creatively. The attention to detail, the noticing of sublime beauty that others might overlook, is beautiful to me. They possess wonderful problem-solving skills and find creative solutions. When I notice this, I can see how this person has connected their mind to their heart, and I'm in awe. I've also witnessed analytical people suffer terribly because their minds have covered over their true self. It's a loss of power over who they truly are.

Incessant thinking is so common that it's difficult to pinpoint, but it will become obvious by the consequences in your life. Do you feel like you are trapped inside an unfulfilled life?

Do you have restless nights? Are your personal relationships being affected? Have you lost your enthusiasm? Everyone has life issues, mostly based on things related to security. We believe we must toss and toil to make things happen, usually by force. There is a better way. This way asks that you begin to trust a higher force who is truly running your life.

Our incessant thoughts do not allow this type of space. They seem to want to protect us but are doing us more harm. They are frustrating our natural flow and cutting us off from our creativity. To stop the harm done by incessant thinking, we need to see in what ways our lives have become unmanageable. As humans, our level of tolerance to pain will vary greatly. It's good to see things in black and white. Writing is an amazing tool that brings many revelations. Walking through the fear of the unknown is one of the strongest ways to convert weakness into strength. When you walk on through to the other side, you will be free.

EXERCISE 1: INCESSANT THOUGHTS RECOGNITION

You may be so accustomed to this type of thinking that it might be difficult to recognize. The spiritual principle behind this exercise is honesty, so you must be rigorously honest with yourself. In your journal, if you have one, or on a blank piece of paper, make a list of five things that demonstrate your automatic responses to incessant thinking. Here is an example:

Non-Serving Actions taken due to my Incessant Thinking

1. *I'm lashing out at my children.*
2. *I'm having trouble getting a full night's rest.*
3. *My mind is always racing.*
4. *I am rarely in the present moment.*
5. *I tend to isolate to not deal with people.*

Next, make a list of five things that demonstrate the consequences you may be facing in your life due to these Non-Serving Actions stemming from incessant thinking. Here is an example.

Incessant Thinking Consequences:

1. *My personal relationships are being affected.*
2. *I am nervous and my health is being affected.*
3. *I feel sadness or depression.*
4. *I don't care about my appearance or am obsessed with it.*
5. *I've lost the inspiration and sense of wonder of being alive.*

SURRENDERING INCESSANT THINKING

If you are in the grips of incessant thinking, the previous exercise will make sense because it is tied to every area of your life. When you are not right with yourself, it's difficult to be right for others. Self-care is especially important. We must make it a habit to discover better tools to help us more easily navigate through life. This is not selfish; it is selfless. You will never show the best version of yourself to others until you first bring out that version in yourself. I don't mean dealing by just plowing through the day, which is often a coverup.

At this point, you may find 101 reasons to justify your incessant thoughts. Don't be deceived, your egoic mind knows you are on to something it does not want you to know. This type of useless thinking needs fuel to maintain itself. There will always be an excuse. Normally it will be relationship, health, or money issues. We all have them, and to some extent, they are meant to be here because they are part of life. The fact we've tried to handle these problems with the wrong tools has only aggravated the issues.

Our egos are fed every time we justify our unconscious actions, thereby fortifying the dysfunction. We must be ready to be stripped of it all. You will not die or disappear. Your problems will probably still be waiting for you. The difference will be how you perceive your challenges, thereby changing the whole dynamic. It will appear as if other people are changing, but it's only you. In changing yourself, you create a chain reaction with far-reaching effects.

Surrendering (giving up) your incessant thinking is only the beginning, but it is crucial. Negative thinking is incessant when it has become so automatic that you have lost control over your choice of thought. If we are to transform our lives, we've got to quit believing things are randomly happening to us. It is not likely we can actualize change unless we take responsibility for the fact that our impulses are contributing to our lives. We have fallen under the illusion we are our thoughts and our minds when, in fact, we are so much more. No wonder your life may be so full of pain and boredom. You may have forgotten who you are. Following the first step is the gateway to freedom—freedom from the bondage of your false self, aka your ego.

Earnestly following these steps will lead you to a spiritual awakening, and you will find your truth within. This inner truth is beyond form; it is our consciousness, and it is where freedom lies. Everything else you've generated in your life—guilt, worry, and fear—came after. These are not your natural states. In truth, you could review your whole life story right now and feel its presence; it is that close, but this is a difficult idea to accept.

Once you have become aware of your incessant negative thoughts, you will be present in the Now. That act of admission will create a wide space, which is the beginning of freedom. By becoming aware, you will have given your ego a major blow. Your ego feeds off of your fears. It pretends to be protecting you from yourself while it is the cause of your troubles. Don't be afraid of your ego; it is *not* your life source, especially if it has exceeded its intended use. Your incessant thoughts will never let you live in the Now and you will miss your life. All the vital functions within your body and the planet are taking place to keep you safe. Millions upon millions of separate functions per nanosecond are ensuring your survival; you and your ego have nothing to do with this. Why not pledge your allegiance to this powerful force instead of your limiting thoughts?

The fact you worry does not make a debt go away, make an illness vanish, or prevent the withdrawal of someone's affection. In fact, it is stealing your energy from the present moment, the only place where change can occur. You cannot create the life of your dreams coming from this place because even though you might reach your goal, you will find it is not enough once you get there. These thoughts are like hungry piranhas that are never satiated.

I used to think if I wasn't always busy, I was missing out on something. I'd become easily bored and restless. This began as a child. I was the oldest child and quite imposing. I was spoiled and always wanted more. I'd watch my little sister, who always seemed so satisfied by any small gesture. I pitied her and wondered how she could be satisfied by so little. Through the years, I realized she had always led a more joyful life than I did and how always needing the next thing to fulfill me was just reaffirming my sense of lack. I lived in my egoic mind and nothing satisfied me for long. Not her; she was happy, and I was the prisoner.

While doing the exercise in this chapter, you may have experienced fear or guilt. Do not let this stop you. Do not worry about what is coming next. This is your ego trying to pull you out of the present moment. All that's being asked of you is to stay in contemplation and look at how your life is being affected by your incessant negative thoughts. It will be easy to see if you observe the consequences. These are simple questions that will require a bit of introspection.

To thine own self be true.

3
CONNECTING WITH YOUR HIGHER POWER

Spiritual Principle: Hope and Faith

> *"Someday, after mastering the winds, the waves, the tides and gravity, we shall harness for God the energies of love, and then, for a second time in the history of the world, man will have discovered fire.'*
>
> —Pierre Teilhard de Chardin

On our quest for freedom, there will be obstacles. Surrendering takes great courage, but there will be even more soul searching and digging needed; for this, we will need power. At this point, we must realize our human power has only gotten us this far. We will need to summon more power. *You must place your will in the hands of a higher power to help you regain your mental freedom.* The great news is it's not far away. It will only take willingness on your part; the rest will unfold naturally for you.

Throughout almost every culture, there is a belief in a powerful divine force that influences our lives. Different "gods" seem to share similar characteristics. I often wondered exactly who God was until I made an awesome discovery that changed my life: I discovered the liberating truth that God can be whomever or whatever we choose it to be. The same can be true for you: God is whomever you say he/she/it is. Whatever your religious inclinations may be and even if you are agnostic or an atheist, this power is working in and through us all. Many people are turned off by the word *God* because it has been tossed around in so many ways that it can have a negative connotation. That's why I use the term *higher power*. The name we give it is incidental, for it's the magnificent powers it bestows we are after.

There is a higher power guiding everything from the cells inside our bodies to the great bodies in the cosmos. There is an innate intelligence governing it all. Whether we acknowledge it or not, it is working on our behalf. We must learn to harness this power and let it work through us. We've invested our faith into dysfunctional systems that are not working. This higher power was here before our thoughts, so it must be greater. Our thoughts could not emerge if not for the underlying power of creation.

If you've wholly surrendered yourself to incessant thinking, you may be beyond human aid; only a power greater than yourself can restore you to sanity by rescuing you from the insanity of a dysfunctional mind. When our life is less than enjoyable and we cannot control our thoughts, we are, to some extent, sick. We are not so different from people who talk to themselves on park benches. Of course, there are different levels of mental disorders, and some people have lost the ability to differentiate true from false. The only difference between us and the person on the park bench is managing to keep our thoughts to ourselves—but we do have the ability to regain our balance when we take the necessary steps to recognize the truth.

Right now, you are having a moment of clarity. This is a miracle. Seize the moment and don't look back. Accept this spiritual solution; help is on its way. Only your spirit is strong enough to break through the conditioned belief systems you have created. You are not those conditioned belief systems, and this is why your higher self will prevail. The mind that created the problem cannot overcome the problem. If reasoning and willpower could have done the job, they would have. Lack of power over your incessant thoughts is your dilemma. You must align yourself with a power greater than yourself to restore you to a peaceful, benevolent state.

Many of us feel abandoned by this power due to the suffering in our lives and in the world. However, at one time or another, I'm sure we have all felt the sense of awe and wonder at how everything in this universe was created. Who made all of this? How are we here? It is obvious to me there is an awesome intelligence in operation. Instead of judging this power as a punishing entity, make it your ally.

We are infinite beings living inside a finite structure, and certain rules govern us. Even though we despise these rules, they create the polarities needed for our material existence. The earth protects us. It shelters us, gives us everything we need—food, water, air, and sunlight. We need these for our bodies to survive, yet our higher self is infinite. They are both part of this creation. Our material and spiritual aspects are a dance of perfect harmony. One complements the other. In our quest for happiness, we have misused one of our most helpful allies—our minds. It's as if the instrument has taken over the operator. What was meant as an instrument of communication for our senses and intuitive thoughts has become our "frenemy." We must come to realize we are not our thoughts; we are not even our minds. We are the operators behind these wonderful tools.

Ask yourself a question: "Who is the thinker behind my thoughts?" Stop for a moment and witness this space. You will confirm there is something infinite within you that is way beyond your thinking mind. We are beautiful paradoxes, infinite beings inside finite structures. Once we learn to connect with our higher selves, we'll come to realize we are the observing witnesses to all that arises in the phenomenal realm. It will then be easier to forge an alliance with a higher power, the power that creates worlds. While part of this power is within us, we are not it entirely. Forging an alliance with a power greater than ourselves is key in helping us navigate through life peacefully and joyfully.

As soon as we are able to lay prejudice aside and have the willingness to believe in a power greater than ourselves, we will begin receiving answers to problems that were once insurmountable.

Creating Your Own Concept of a Higher Power

You do not have to accept anyone's concept of a higher power. You can create your own concept. You don't have to let any type of prejudice get in your way of forging a relationship with a higher power. Don't do yourself the disservice of ignoring this power only because you've been turned off by someone else's conception of it. GOD can simply stand for "Good Orderly Direction."

Knowing I could create my own concept of God was a liberating invitation. I'd always rebelled at the thought of a God who would punish us for our sins. I was taught we were sinners and evil at our core. This did not jive with what, as a child, I intuitively knew. Deep inside, I naturally felt God was good and we are innately good and benign. Yes, there was pain in the world—as years passed, I felt it more acutely—but I saw clearly how there was much more love in the world than hate. My innate knowing was incongruent with the God I was being taught to fear.

I was taking classes for my first communion when I was presented once more with the idea we were sinners, so I asked my mom about it. She gave me the greatest gift that day with words of wisdom: She told me not to worry about what the priest said, that God is always good and would *always* forgive us. This was what I genuinely wanted to hear, so I believed her. That was the power of belief in action. I decided to ignore the negative and instead focus on the love. Many things have happened since those early days, but the seed was planted, and it is the same seed I am planting in you.

FAITH IN SOMETHING GREATER

An awesome power is at arm's reach, but you must accept it. This power is always working and governs all of life. Do not let the stigma of the word *God* drive you toward a lifetime of alienation from this magnificent force. It is part of you, but while we are identified with our ego, we must place our faith in something outside of us that is greater than us. It is obvious how at this point we have not mustered the will to change on our own. Admitting this will open the gateway for power to flood through you.

We each get to live this life and choose where to align our powers. This is because there is great power inside us since we are all part of creation. We have amazing creative abilities, but this power is trapped beneath layers of conditioned responses that no longer serve us. These too are powers, but they are the wrong kind of power. We have given these illusions and fears powers that do not belong to them. They will live in our minds and our bodies and manifest as tension and ulcers. The power of belief is an amazing thing. In my experience, it's the most powerful power of all. Any thought you solidify into a belief will become real to you. As real as your incessant thoughts may seem, they are not; you just believe them to be.

Events manifest as your life situation, but you are not bound to them because naturally, you are beautiful and free. There is a subtle presence within you that can choose to align itself with a higher power. It knows nothing of suffering and strife. The moment you can humble yourself and admit that, on your own, you cannot overcome certain difficulties, that presence will be ready to say yes. The door of your mind may shut many times at the thought of this type of surrender, but it's where your freedom lies.

There is a reason the exercise in this chapter comes after the first and why all the chapters are in this particular order. The first exercise was based on surrender and honesty. You must surrender in order to reconstruct. The second exercise is based on hope and faith. The reason you are here is because you deserve a better life and you know it: You have hope and faith!

Try not to be cynical. Give this spiritual side of life a fair chance. This exercise will be a great relief in your life, and it will humble you in a beautiful way. Life is harsh when you carry it on your back like a rock. Surrender to the belief there is invisible power to aide you. You don't have to do this alone. If you have never thought of the concept of creating your own higher power, it may feel unnatural. While it is true we are all ultimately working with the same force, the ways we harness this power are individual; your concept will be unique to you. This will make it more special and help you create a safe alliance with this force.

I felt compelled to write this book because I wanted to share the freedom I found by accepting these principles. If the idea of a God or a higher power is unacceptable, take heart in the belief these spiritual principles have worked in hundreds of thousands of people's lives. They are the same principles used in 12-step programs around the world. They have helped many gain freedom from drugs, alcohol, food, and sex, which can be some of life's most destructive forces. They are the ultimate outlets of desperation we turn to as human beings. If these principles can work on such extreme cases, they can also work for you. All you must do is find a belief in a power greater than yourself that will relieve you of the incessant negative thinking that is creating dysfunction in your life.

Isn't it exciting to know you can formulate your own concept of the divine? Take all the powerful beliefs that ring true and focus them on the belief of a benign power—one that is personal to you and will be your guiding light. We are not meant to be in isolation, alone and totally unaware of this vital force that is already within us. Aligning with this force will be the most powerful thing you will ever do. It will walk with you every step of the way, but you must believe. It is my goal to lead you to the principle behind each step. Spiritual principles don't change as words and techniques do. They are set in place to create harmony and balance in our world. I am attempting to guide you and show you how these exercises worked for me; however, these are only pointers. The principles of hope and faith are universal. There is no wrong way to discover them.

Until now, we have been worshipping our minds. Although it seems like a convincing proposition, we've forgotten how our mind is only a tool meant to be used by us. Instead, it has been using us. There is immense power within us and it is not exclusively the power of our thoughts. It is the conscious awareness within us that holds great power. To make this realization, we must first surrender our loyalty to our incessant thinking; otherwise, we will continue to experience the same fate.

> *"For faith in a power greater than ourselves, and miraculous demonstrations of that power in human lives, are facts as old as man himself."*
>
> —*Alcoholics Anonymous: The Big Book*

EXERCISE 2: PART A—ALLIANCE WITH YOUR HIGHER POWER

You can take action to create an alliance with your higher power. I'm a firm believer that if you bring your body, your mind will follow. Taking physical steps has always helped me on my spiritual journey. The following is one of the assignments that truly helped me early on. I was guided to write a list of ten attributes I would assign my higher power. In your journal, if you have one, or on a blank piece of paper, simply make a list of ten attributes you wish your higher power possessed. My list went something like this:

Loving
Forgiving
Powerful
Graceful
Empowering
Patient
Wise
Reliable
Strong
Omnipresent

The goal is to form a relationship with a power you will come to rely on. It is not easy forging a relationship with an invisible power. This exercise might seem overly simplistic, but it will help you envision the perfect ideal of your higher power. It will exert your willingness and desire to make contact.

As you make your list, bring up any memories you may have of this power. Look at nature and be in awe of the sacred geometry and all the naturally occurring forces needed to hold everything together. Think of your loved ones and notice how this deep feeling of love could have never been fabricated by your mind. Take a moment to think about your heart pumping and your lungs breathing. Notice all the vital functions taking place in life in which you don't have to play a conscious role. Remind yourself of the magnificence of the mountains and power of the oceans. Think about how animals instinctively take care of themselves, sometimes traveling vast distances in great migrations. One has to wonder at how all this was encoded. There *is* an awesome power guiding all. One day science and religion will join hands. I believe science is humanity's best effort to explain the laws imparted by a higher power.

For the most part, each of us goes through life trying to do the best we can. We depend on our human will to get us through our day. The human will is a beautiful power, but it has its limitations. We can get much more accomplished through a combination of inspiration, spontaneous action, and work than we can with work alone. As you begin to tap into the guidance of your higher power, you will notice a gentle flow guiding you. You won't feel all alone in a hostile world; you will come to understand there is a powerful force by your side ready to help.

In the second part of this exercise, you will be asked to go deeper. *You must be willing to turn your will over to the care of your higher power.* Now that you've come to believe in a power greater than yourself with whom you may align yourself, you must be willing to take it further. Your higher power will be of maximum benefit to you once you align yourself with its guidance. You may be wondering, "How exactly can I turn my will and my life over to the care of my higher power?" Well, you do this through the power of belief. You must be willing to make the decision to turn your life and your will over to its care. This is not a one-time event; you must make the decision on a daily basis and be ready to receive guidance. You will not lose yourself in the process, but you will lose the parts of yourself that are getting in your way, especially the repetitive, useless patterns. As mentioned, the key to unlock the door of this type of freedom is willingness. This is all you will need to help you through. This step may seem unnatural and go against the very grain of your will. However, it is the crux of the whole system, for turning your will over to the care of your higher power will unleash a wealth of spiritual power.

You will not be so easily burdened by trivial things because you will know there is something more powerful handling things for you. You will begin to lose fear of things and people. You will begin to realize how this power is doing for you what you could not do for yourself. But you *must* take action. This is not a passive idea; it's an active step, and it calls for your action every day.

EXERCISE 2: PART B—TURNING YOUR WILL OVER TO YOUR HIGHER POWER

In the morning, before you get out of bed, begin by asking your higher power to guide your steps for the day, to help you see things with new eyes, the way it would have you see them. Although we worship our human vision, it is very limited. There are thousands of combinations in the form of solutions to our problems, but when we are thinking through our limited minds, we become fixated on just a few solutions, ones that may not be nearly as effective as the ones our higher power can see. Realize that by making a commitment to work the exercises in this book, you've already decided to turn your will and your life to its care in a sense.

The reason I suggest turning your will over to the care of your higher power each morning is so you can get ahead of yourself in the sense of learning to align yourself before starting your day, before other influences have chance to penetrate your mind. Remember that turning your will over is not a one-time event. You must do it over and over throughout the day each time you need guidance. As part of my daily routine, I turn my will over to my higher power every morning. I was taught this beautiful prayer, and I believe it will work for you.

Morning Prayer to Turn Your Will Over: *Higher Power, I offer my incessant negative thoughts to you. Please guide me and direct my thinking toward your truth. Relieve me of my obsessive mind that I may better follow your guidance. Please take away my difficulties so peace and clarity of mind may be the living proof of your strength. Please help me be an example of your power, of your love, and of your way of life.*

This is a great way to start the day. There will be days when it will be easy, but there will be other days when your thoughts will attack with full force. On the days when it is hard to turn your will over to your higher power, especially on those days when a specific fear or worry overtakes you, you can use another valuable tool I call my HP Box (Higher Power Box; see Exercise 2: Part C).

I understand it is a tall order to turn your will and life over to the care of your higher power as you understand it on a daily basis, but it's absolutely necessary for the miracle of freedom from the bondage of ego. You will not disappear into thin air by turning your will over. Instead, you will be squashing your ego, the part of your mind that has turned against itself. It's the part of you that believes it has all the answers and knows best. It is also the part of you that can never be free due to its fear of death. You must be free of it because it is the reason for your unhappiness. Your ego will not be happy once it realizes it is being challenged on this level. The truth is, it is only a shadow, an illusion of you who you truly are—it is *not* in charge.

Your ego will throw all kinds of punches at you in the forms of fear and even threats. It does not want to lose its host. Don't be afraid. Have faith and keep your alliance with your loving power that knows nothing of fear and loss. Yes, there is a place for everything, and you will have an ego self as long as you have a body, but you must dwell in the sunlight of the spirit and visit the ego self only as needed. In time, your ego will merge with your true self and become your ally. I understand this can be frightening and will take courage to acknowledge, but humanity needs you to awaken from this trance. We each need to come to this awareness as soon as possible. It will occur one person at a time. Each of us is a miracle, a gift of existence.

EXERCISE 2: PART C—CREATING YOUR HP BOX

The purpose of an HP (Higher Power) Box is to create a physical object into which you can release a fear, worry, or concern. As I stated earlier, if you bring your body, your mind will follow. Creating an HP Box is a beautiful way to make a stronger bond with your higher power and, most important, to release the negative energy and fear that paralyze you when you are most afraid. When you are paralyzed by fear or are uncertain about a decision you must make, simply write out your fear, worry, or concern on piece of paper and turn it over to your higher power by releasing it into the HP Box.

The act of writing out your fear on paper and removing it from your mind will cause the trouble to lose momentum. You will break the incessant stream of thoughts. Second, by having the faith to turn it over to your higher power, relief will come. Then you will come to realize how your higher power is doing for you what you could not do for yourself.

You can create an HP Box out of any item you wish. For instance, my first HP Box was a shoebox. I've since gotten a beautiful wooden box I've decorated with little stones. The power is not in the box, but in the faith you have while you are releasing your troubles. It is your trust that your higher power will handle things for you. As I mentioned earlier, thoughts contain power and frequencies. That's why we feel better after talking out our problems with our friends. By expressing your feelings and not bottling them up, your problems lose power. I love to write; I find it to be a great tool. The notes I write and release into my HP Box look something like this:

Dear Higher Power,

I turn over the fear of not meeting my sales quota this month. I release all the fear and anxiety I am feeling. Please take this over so I may sleep soundly. I love you. Thanks.

Sandra

When I first began to use my HP Box, the process seemed unnatural. I could not see how this would work, but I tried it, and after a few tries, it began to work. I began to notice a sense of ease and relief as I wrote my dilemma and surrendered it to my HP Box. As I delivered each offering, I would make the decision to know and trust it would be handled for me. Turning my dilemma over was a relief I could sometimes feel physically. In time, I would go back to my HP Box and look at the petitions I'd offered in the past, and I would find to my satisfaction that most of my dilemmas had been resolved favorably, and the ones that didn't turn out as I wished were nonetheless resolved.

Don't ever give up until the miracle happens. There is a saying, *fake it till you make it*. There is truth to this. Things will sometimes feel "fake" or uncomfortable because you've never done them before. You are creating mental rearrangements and psychic changes that will serve you better. Many things don't feel real when we first try them. Can you remember learning to ride a bike or speak in public? Or, if you have children, even being a parent might have felt unreal in the beginning. Today I like to say, "Do it until it becomes real." In some cases, you might get instant relief by taking this action the first time, but it might take a little while. Give it a chance and don't quit. I did it until it became real and now it has helped me live a more satisfying life.

Faith That Works

You will need much willingness and persistence to cultivate faith and make it a working part of your mind. I am not referring to wishful thinking, which is vague and superficial. I am talking about a faith that works. It has been my experience that for faith to become powerful, you must abandon yourself to a deep knowing that things will turn out well, a knowing that something has your back, that there is a force backing you. I believe many of us know this at a deep level, but fear paralyzes us. Remember that faith without work is dead, so it is essential to practice these exercises daily. You will soon realize how your dependence on your higher power is your chief source of strength. Be aware you are already turning your life and your will over to your higher power just by making the decision to embark on this journey. The rest of this book and the remaining exercises will work based on your willingness. This will then be a beautiful blessing in your life.

In the next chapter, you will learn how our natural instincts have fallen out of balance, thereby causing many of the troubles in our lives. At this point, it is essential to have faith in your higher power to guide you through the following exercises. Congratulations on coming this far!

4

FORGIVING YOUR DREAM CRUSHERS

Spiritual Principle: Courage

"Forgiveness is the fragrance that the violet sheds on the heel that has crushed it."

—Mark Twain

Our egos arise from our primary impulses, our natural instincts. The ego is not the problem; the problem is how our instincts have become exaggerated and harmful. As human beings, we need the right amount of fear and desire, but our over-identification with the body and mind is what creates such polar extremes.

Striving to achieve greater heights while following our passions is a marvelous course of action, but when it becomes fierce competition at the expense of our personal relationships, we have a problem. I believe the desire for material things to experience life at greater heights is admirable, but when we are so consumed by the material world that we are driven to live beyond our means and are out of touch with our reality, something is not right. When engaging in immoral or unethical business becomes something to consider, we have become completely out of balance.

The desire for sex, relationships, and material and emotional security are inherent in humanity. Yet these instincts have become the end result instead of the means to the end. What was intended as a useful tool to help us meet our natural desires can turn into disease, strife, and disharmony in our relationships. These "human desires" are means to deeper truths that speak of connection, love, sharing, and creating. They are instruments that help guide us toward higher vibrations that fill us with joy, love, and bliss. The acts in of themselves can never fulfill these higher states.

In an attempt for freedom, we take on increased responsibilities day after day, while missing out on our lives and deeper connections. It's difficult to have a creative life when we are constantly running on stress hormones. Most of our emotional problems have been a case of misdirected instinct. When this occurs, our wonderful inborn instincts turn into liabilities. Because everyone is running on the same fear-based fuel, we are unknowingly (and sometimes knowingly) inflicting great amounts of pain on each other. The intensity of the harm we cause one another varies from mild to extreme. Because we are possessed by the stress chemicals created by our incessant thoughts, we are operating mostly in a state of fight or flight. This creates distance from our human companions, and we secretly live in fear and mistrust of one another. This is all happening on autopilot, but if you create a time gap by being still in the present moment, you can see your uncontrollable thoughts moving by. When you see this, notice how you are not any of those thoughts—that you are the observer watching them move by, like clouds.

THE ENERGY OF EMOTIONS

Anger is a natural emotion we feel any time there is an injustice, whether real or perceived. Anytime an event happens where we were treated unjustly, anger will occur. Anger is a very natural response. The problem is that most of us haven't been taught how to process this natural response. Most of us have never been taught the deep aspects of being human. You don't know what you don't know. We've learned to either lash out or stuff it in. Anger then turns into resentment, one that we can carry for a lifetime. This pent-up resentment will eat up our creativity, happiness, and freedom. A strong enough resentment can make us very sick. Many times we will carry justified resentments and then feel guilty because of it.

We work hard at keeping these feelings at bay. They can become lodged in our subconscious minds to the point we may be in denial that they are even there. It's a form of energy that was never converted into a valuable lesson. There will always be life events that will make us angry, but we must learn to direct this energy in a positive way. Otherwise, it can become part of our personalities.

Anger can become chronic to the point we can't even identify it. It may have started by an injustice. If time has passed and you've never released this energy, it will creep into other areas of your life. But of all the instincts we've misused, fear trumps them all. Fear in the form of instinct is needed for self-preservation, but we've used it beyond its intended purpose. Many of us live in fear of the unknown, financial fear, and fear of people and of their opinions. This is why we isolate, pretend we are someone we are not, and feel inadequate. We are afraid of people's opinions, of being judged, and of not being good enough.

I used to lie to myself, believing I didn't care what other people thought of me. It was mostly an excuse to act out, but it was also an attempt to convince myself it really didn't matter when it did. Deep inside, we all want to feel we are doing the right thing; we are all connected to one another. Other people really represent other aspects of us. We are like mirrors, reflecting back all that we express into the world.

In our journey toward spiritual growth, we will stop contributing to the accumulation of negativity in our minds and bodies, but residue from the past still lives. You do have the power to drop everything in this very moment, notice your true presence within, and be done with it. But not everyone has the willingness for this type of liberation. For many of us, it comes in increments. We don't have to spend our whole lives in this process. Once you've made enough space for the sunlight of the spirit to shine through, you will make progress in leaps and bounds. As eternal beings, I don't believe we ever stop growing. So let's enjoy the ride.

How to Recognize Anger and Other Emotions

Before we can deal with our anger, we must recognize why we are angry and allow ourselves the freedom to feel it. Our society tells us not to feel. We quickly dig into our denial toolkit and reach for something, often outside of ourselves, to soothe us. It is important to recognize it is best to deal with anger sooner than later. Waiting too long to deal with anger makes us vulnerable: we think it has gone away, but it has only been covered over, and after a few days this unresolved anger gets buried alive in our subconscious. We will no longer remember what we should have dealt with, but the anger is still there. Just because it's been tucked away does not mean it disappeared. It has now been transformed into resentment. Once this process has occurred, it becomes increasingly difficult to undo. Our denial systems kick in and create an array of disguises. Then, one fine day, we will act "out of character" over something seemingly insignificant and will wonder where our reaction came from.

To recognize anger or any of our emotions, we must learn to sit with them for a while. They are messengers trying to communicate. Our society has become one of little emotional intelligence. We quickly try to overanalyze and dissect the feeling, a feeling that is only trying to be felt. It's an expression from a deep part within us. Why would we want to constantly drown them out? I am not asking you to turn it into a pity party or punish yourself; I am simply saying we need to allow our feelings to be acknowledged.

Many times, we don't even realize we are angry because we've been trained to shut off our perception of it. You must learn to listen to your warning signals, which come in the form of feelings. Because feelings are a form of energy expressed in your body, you can always notice them. Next time you are becoming agitated, notice your feeling inside your body. It might manifest as tightness in your chest or in your gut. You might feel your shoulders tense up or notice your heart begin to palpitate. These are all signs you've signaled some type of stress in your body. When this happens, stop and notice where you are feeling it. Acknowledge it's happening and just sit with it for a few minutes. You will then have created space, breaking the stream of thought and helping it lose momentum. This is a simple exercise. By creating space between the thought and the feeling, you will most likely have a better response toward the situation. You can then make a better choice to create an improved outcome.

We've been taught to believe that because anger doesn't feel good, it is not okay to feel it. Then there are those who don't even know they are angry, but one glance will convince you it has become a part of their character. Simply bringing awareness to an episode of anger will help you diffuse this strong negative charge. Next time you become angry, remember to notice where inside your body you are feeling this anger. It sounds counterintuitive, but noticing where we feel anger can help us dispel it, and it works like magic.

We must learn to honor every part of ourselves, including our anger. When we reject parts of ourselves, we make them into enemies when they should all be allies. If you have enough awareness to simply identify anger being manifested in your body, you will create space between your anger and yourself. This awareness will prevent you from being completely high-jacked by the emotion, and it will allow you the milliseconds needed to make a better choice. This may simply be taking a deep breath or going for a walk. This is progress and a wonderful exercise in concentration that can change many outcomes. You will stop reacting and begin responding. The big picture is a collage of little victories. The thoughts and actions you make will influence you in this lifetime and beyond.

As you begin to make room, you will allow the sunlight of the spirit to become your guiding light. You will begin to vibrate at a higher frequency and receive answers to questions that used to baffle you. You will become a conscious participant in the evolution of the universe. Make this a practice, and you will be pleased. Yes, there are many exercises and techniques on creativity and manifestation, but I have found that unless I was willing to acknowledge my anger and resentments and clear away the baggage they caused, I did not have enough energy to become a conscious creator. We expend tremendous amounts of energy keeping past memories tucked away.

Releasing Stagnant Energy

The exercise to follow will help you unleash all the stagnant energy stored in the form of guilt, resentments, and fears that keep you anchored to the past. No one wants to relive unpleasant events from our past, but if we genuinely want what we say we want, this is a crucial exercise. Don't spend unnecessary years of your life practicing spiritual techniques and "not getting it." I urge you to tackle this head-on. Strike while the iron is hot!

Something has guided you this far because something has made sense for you. We are all on different journeys toward the same destination. If you are ready to make a dramatic change in your life, this exercise is for you. Remember, there is a reason the exercises in this book are in a particular order; please don't skip around. You were first asked to become fully aware of your incessant negative thoughts. Then, you were asked to find a power greater than yourself that can restore you to balance and be willing to turn your life and your will over to its care. You will need this force as an ally on this journey.

Now, you will perform an internal housecleaning. The spiritual principle behind this exercise is courage. Courage doesn't mean we don't feel fear. It means we act despite being afraid. We act because there is a reward greater than the uncertainty we must encounter. To have extraordinary results, we must put in extraordinary effort. Most people don't ever consider doing a personal inventory or housecleaning of this type. The ones who do are usually people who have been beaten into submission due to the agony of addictions to drugs, food, alcohol, or sex. Once I had the honor of working these steps and witnessed the miraculous changes in my life, I began to understand how everyone can make use of them.

The truth is that only a few people will muster the courage to take the actions necessary to bring about a spiritual awakening. If you are simply getting by and you feel it is "not so bad," you may be tempted to skip this vital step. Only the ones who deeply, truly desire a new life as do the sick and dying will have enough willingness to succeed. It is my wish you will be among the few.

EXERCISE 3: PART A—HOUSECLEANING

This exercise calls for you to *make an honest inventory of yourself.*

You must launch on a vigorous course of action to be rid of your resentments. Most of us are carrying resentments from our past, which takes a great amount of energy. This is energy we need to release to become more creative and find our life purpose. You might think you don't have any resentments but think again. Resentments may be directed toward institutions, religions, politics, and even ourselves. They can be directed at people from our past, our bosses, close friends, and relatives. Some may even be innocent bystanders.

You will need to practice courage and honesty for this exercise. Don't be ashamed; this is your chance to let it all out. If there is an event from your past that still bothers you, it still holds energy. For your inventory, you will make three columns in your journal, if you have one, or on a blank piece of paper as follows:

Who/What I Am Resenting	The Cause of My Resentment	Affects My...

When we are hurt, the hurt will usually take on one of the following four forms of fears because hurt is almost always fear-based:

- **Financial:** When we fear not getting something material we want or fear losing what we already have.
- **Emotional:** When we are affected at an emotional level. This can show up as feelings of low self-esteem, trust issues, jealousy or security issues, and feelings

of abandonment. Emotional fears can manifest in many forms.
- **Societal:** When we worry about what society thinks of us or about how they judge us according to the actions we take or fail to take.
- **Sexual:** When our sex life is in jeopardy or we feel threatened by it.

Here's an example:

Who/What I Am Resenting	The Cause of My Resentment	Affects My…
My mom	She didn't let me take singing lessons as a child.	Emotional and societal well-being.
My boyfriend	He's controlling and doesn't let me be me.	Emotional, financial, societal, and sexual well-being.
My boss	He's unpredictable and inconsiderate.	Financial, emotional, and societal well-being
My brother	He only calls when he needs something.	Emotional and financial well-being.
The government	They overtax us and keep secrets.	Financial and societal well-being.
The Bible	It's extremely negative; I see a punishing God.	Emotional and societal well-being.

A life filled with resentments can never lead to freedom. If we are to live joyful lives, we must take action. Simply wishing for change is ineffective. When we harbor such feelings, we shut ourselves from the sunlight of the spirit and risk losing our zeal for life. When we hold on to grudges, we continue to live in the past. Taking pen to paper will shed light on hidden ghosts. They will then begin to lose power and there will be room for new experiences in real time. To reach the depth of your soul, you must clear out the baggage.

Once you have completed your list, you may get a sudden feeling of relief. Perhaps you feel anger, or nothing at all. Every case is a good case because you have had the courage to put your effort into it. You will have demonstrated to your higher self that you want this and are a willing to go to any length to get it.

So far you have practiced the following spiritual principles:

1. Honesty
2. Hope
3. Faith
4. Courage

This is worth more than gold. I sincerely congratulate you! Move on, brave one. Your freedom lies ahead!

Beyond this place of wrath and tears
Looms but the horror of the shade,
And yet the menace of the years
Finds and shall find me unafraid.

It matters not how strait the gate,
How charged with punishments the scroll,
I am the master of my fate,
I am the captain of my soul.
Invictus

—Excerpted from "Invictus" by William Ernest Henley

Finding Forgiveness

It is clear we must first be rid of resentments to re-create our lives, but how? How can we come to terms with the negative events and people who have inflicted pain on us? The first thing we must realize is that these people were spiritually sick. Though we do not like their symptoms or how they affected us, it's important to understand how they simply did not have enough consciousness to do better at the time. The type of sickness I am referring to is emotional and spiritual imbalance. What I mean by this is that most of the people roaming in society are plagued by tormentors in their minds. Everyone is trying to run the show while ignorant of their true natures. Although what others did hurt us, we must learn to set them free so we may in turn free ourselves. The fact you are reading these words says you are more spiritually advanced than a large percentage of the population. Making spiritual growth a priority takes wisdom.

One of the definitions for *unforgiveness* is "having or making no allowance for error or weakness." When people act unfairly toward us, it means they are in a sense of error or weakness. They've become disconnected from their true natures and have gone numb. I understand there are varying types of harms done to us and how some may seem unforgivable, but the truth is that until we can forgive, we will not be free. As human beings, we all make mistakes. There must be a case where you can remember treating someone poorly. We've all done it, but it hurts more when it is done to us. When we hold on to resentment, we're drinking poison, hoping the other will die.

If someone harmed you as a child and you can't think of any possible offense on your side, you can write down your inability to forgive as your current part in the matter. Making the decision to take ownership of the fact you hold resentment is a major step toward healing. Your forgiveness will set you free from reliving the past event or transgression in your mind. You can't change the past, but you can affect your future. You will see how your experience can one day help others. This does not excuse the bad behavior done to you. Let the natural laws of the universe take care of that for you. Eventually, a balance is always struck through the laws of causation, or cause and effect. Be brave and cut your offender loose. Your only part in the matter may be your lack of forgiveness. It will be scary to forgive, but the amount of freedom you will gain will be priceless.

At the top of my resentment list was my mother. My great friend and mentor used to say, "If it's not one thing, it's my mother," and this was exactly my case. It was quite difficult to see my part in the matter. As a child, all I ever wanted to do was sing. Because of her own fear, my mother did not help me carry out my desire. I carried resentment around for years, to the point I lost my singing voice. While it's true it was not my fault my mother did not honor my passion as an aspiring singer, the way I treated her after that was unacceptable. I began to mistrust her and even started hating her. I rebelled, and it cost us both many tears. My role in the matter was my rebellious and hurtful nature toward her.

Down the list in my example, you can see where I wrote "the government." At the time I wrote my list, I was behind on my taxes and thought the interest and fees were ridiculous. I decided not to pay and live in denial, and the bills multiplied. I realized as I wrote my list that my failure to take action was truly my mistake.

I lived in denial and nonacceptance. Regarding my Bible resentment, I realized I'd never given the Bible a fair chance. While I didn't agree with all of its teachings, there is great wisdom within. I don't consider myself to be a typical Christian, as I practice my own conception of God, but one of my favorite prayers is the Lord's Prayer. There's a beautiful book written by Emmet Fox called *The Sermon on the Mount*. In this book, Fox interprets the meaning of the Lord's Prayer in a fascinating way that enabled me to easily grasp the concepts of the teachings of Christ. "Forgive us our trespasses as we forgive those who trespass against us." This clause in the Lord's Prayer emphasizes the importance of forgiveness. It clearly states we must forgive others if we are expecting to be forgiven. It is counterintuitive, but if we hold someone in bondage of unforgiveness, we are energetically binding ourselves to this person, place, or event. We will not be free or forgiven until we can release the offender.

Fox goes on to say, "The forgiveness of sins is the central problem of life. Sin is a sense of separation from God, and is the major tragedy of human experience. It is, of course, rooted in selfishness." Further, he says, "Notice that Jesus does not say, 'forgive me my trespasses and I will try to forgive others,' or 'I will see if it can be done, or 'I will forgive generally, with certain exceptions.' He obliges us to declare that we have actually forgiven, and forgiven all, and he makes our claim to our own forgiveness to depend upon that."

I can't overemphasize the importance of forgiveness on our journey toward spiritual growth. In life, at some point, we all play the role of victim and oppressor. Your oppressor was once someone's victim. We may have a long line of victims ourselves. It took years for me to consider and realize how many people I had hurt. When we choose to forgive, we break the cycle and true healing takes place. This is what the world needs most.

EXERCISE 3: PART B—HOUSECLEANING

As the final part of this exercise, I will ask you to include a fourth column, which is a particularly important part of the exercise. This is an interesting column as you will be able to observe your part in how your life unfolded. If something affects us, we've played a role in the dilemma. Until we can see our part, we cannot initiate change. Here's my example from earlier with the addition of the fourth column:

Who/What I Am Resenting	The Cause of My Resentment	Affects My...	My Wrongs
My mom	She didn't let me take singing lessons as a child.	Emotional and societal well-being.	I treated her badly thereafter; I would defy her and became disrespectful.
My boyfriend	He's controlling and doesn't let me be me.	Emotional, financial, societal, and sexual well-being.	I mistreated him and belittled him. I was dishonest and cruel.
My boss	He's unpredictable and inconsiderate.	Financial, emotional, and societal well-being	I was inconsiderate and worked just enough to get by. I tapped into the business account.
My brother	He only calls when he needs something.	Emotional and financial well-being.	I only called him when I needed something. I was not honest about how I felt about our relationship.
The government	They overtax us and keep secrets.	Financial and societal well-being.	I became cynical, caused discord instead of harmony, and became alienated.
The Bible	It's extremely negative; I see a punishing God.	Emotional and societal well-being.	I became close-minded and cynical and judged people I considered "Bible thumpers."

All these exercises go contrary to our natural desires because they work toward ego deflation, and this exercise is no different. Taking pen to paper and admitting to our higher power and to ourselves our resentments and wrongs is a huge step, but I will ask you to go one step further. This is perhaps the most difficult of all the exercises. When writing this book, I was tempted to leave this exercise out, but I later realized you would not get the benefit of a deep transformation unless you follow all the steps I followed.

EXERCISE 3: PART C—CONFESSION

We are all on different spiritual journeys, but we all want joy and freedom. While our journeys may be different, our suffering in one form or another is the same. Who am I to say my pain was worse than someone else's? I will not skimp on any steps, for I wish you the same amount of joy and freedom given me. It's important to admit our wrongs to ourselves and to a higher power. The moment we begin, the denial systems we've created begin losing power, but there is something even more amazing that happens when we admit to another the nature of our wrongs. Here we begin to unleash enormous amounts of healing power.

An Important Step Toward Liberation

Throughout history, "confession" has been used as a form of atonement, but it is not only because it has been written in sacred texts that we reap the benefits. It is the transmutation of energy that takes place each time a phenomenon of confession occurs. The moment we are willing to release pent-up energy in the form of secrets, we unleash a major creative force previously suppressed. When we suppress secrets about ourselves, we are sabotaging our existence every step of the way because creative energy is sacrificed to keep negative memories at bay. We all have secrets, and there are things about ourselves we may think we can never share with another human. It's a great act of courage to embrace this part of your spiritual development.

When we confess and are able to finally release the parts of ourselves no longer serving us, we are telling the universe we are now ready to move on. It is the beginning of the end of living in the past, and this transmutation of energy will turn into courage. Our bodies might be scared to take this step, but our hearts and souls will be released. The open expression of our new insights will signal the universe how we've matured beyond foolish fear and are now ready to move beyond it. It will squash our ego and allow our spirit room for expansion. This is why your ego will resist this exercise the most. Your ego will try to convince you it is totally unnecessary, but do not be deceived.

This is one of the most important steps toward liberation. The wear and tear of keeping secrets is not worth living. Remember, everything around us is composed of energy and keeping secrets takes energy. Once you've released this heaviness, you will unleash surges of energy you can use to create a new life.

> *"If you want to find the secrets of the universe,*
> *think in terms of energy, frequency and vibration."*
>
> —Nikola Tesla

Our soul's integrity should be the primary purpose of our lives because it is from this place that we can reap the fruits of the spirit. Here lies an endless spring of good. If we are to wake up from the fog of deception, we must be willing to make our spiritual restoration our top priority. We must be willing to give up anything standing in our way, and that means our secrets. Your secrets have already been exposed after working the previous exercises in this chapter. Go back to your list and take a look at the fourth column. Notice the patterns in your behavior and actions. If you were honest, light will be shed on things you never noticed.

If we continue to run from our problems in life, we will meet them again around the corner in a new guise. As humans, this is a fundamental truth for us all. Once you have a burning desire to be free, you will be able to take this liberating step.

A confession does not mean you have to share your secret with the victim of the secret or with the police. It means you need to release this energy in the form of a confession to another human being. This can be a stranger or a close friend. We would not want to make matters worse by talking to our partners about being unfaithful or our bosses about tapping into the business account. We would probably cause further damage by taking such actions. You can choose a spiritual advisor, priest, rabbi, or a trusted friend (someone who is neutral) to confess to.

When you are ready, you can express to your confidant how you have decided to take a new path in your life and how this calls for you to take certain actions. Express your gratitude for the ability to be open and trusting with the person and assure them this has nothing to do with them, that they are serving as your confidant on this important part of your journey. Always be thankful.

If your secret has legal implications, you might want to speak to a lawyer or a priest. Make sure you will not cause any further damage. Normally, you cannot be of service to others if you are behind bars, although there are some exceptions. If your secret is something overly complicated along those lines, you may want to turn it over to your higher power for further guidance. If you do this earnestly, the answers will come. Sometimes we feel guilty over thoughts in our heads. Just because we have not played out our thoughts does not mean they are not taking up room in our mind; these too must go. As I said earlier, we are not our thoughts, but one of the ego's most clever disguises is to make us believe we *are* them. If you have had a recurring thought about something that does not gladden you, take this time to get it out. You may never do this again, so now is your chance. Again, strike while the iron is hot.

We want to release our souls. We are on a mission to make peace with ourselves. By covering up the things we are not proud of within ourselves, we create separation from our higher self. We become fragmented. This is high maintenance and unsustainable. The depletion of energy will show up in our lives as a disease or a low-quality life. If we create this type of separation within ourselves, how are we supposed to be real with others? Never be afraid of being completely honest with yourself. Your freedom and joy depend on it. Our secrets and our guilt are no longer true for us. They are only lessons based on actions from the past. By taking this new action, we will be in the furthest place from denial. You must become ever more conscious of your actions and always be grateful there are ways to mitigate errors and be free.

5
REARRANGING YOUR CHARACTER

Spiritual Principles: Willingness and Humility

"We come nearest to the great when we are great in humility."

—Rabindranath Tagore

Continuing to run from other people, places, or things in the form of denial or arrogance is not the answer. When we don't get to the cause of our problems, we are bound to perpetuate our mistakes. There are forces at play that have been embedded in our personalities by repetition; these are our character flaws.

They are the reasons we keep picking the same types of partners or bosses. The problem is we cannot see them, only their effects. Just like the eye cannot see itself, the knife cannot cut itself, or the hand cannot write itself, we cannot see what we are. What we can see are the consequences of events continuing to show up in our lives. Once we begin to make a habit of using the outside world as a reflection of ourselves, we will become wise in a short amount of time. Anytime you are having uncomfortable feelings, it's usually signaling growth can occur. You can choose to walk through it or turn from it. You must learn to see yourself *as you are* and not as you *think* you are.

What Are Character Flaws?

A flaw is simply a shortcoming or imperfection. I was taught that these counterproductive tendencies are called our character flaws. They are characteristics that have become our *modus operandi*. They may have worked for us at some point but no longer serve our spiritual evolution. Before we can transmute these forces, we must first find out what they are.

These characteristics arise out of an exaggeration of our inborn instincts. We will reach a point in our earthly journey where our spiritual development will no longer be a mere wish but the most necessary ingredient for profound happiness. No amount of money or power will satisfy this deep yearning. In this moment, we will wish for the conditions in our lives to change, enabling something new to shine forth, "something" we do not yet understand. We shall then pray to our higher power for a change in the conditions of our hearts and minds that will affect the outcome of our reality.

It is obvious that to get a different result we must change the cause, but its application is not so easy. The result of all the unfavorable circumstances in our lives arises from the negative conditions we've programmed within ourselves. These negative tools and attitudes are also our character flaws. No matter what happens on this journey, we must learn always to be gentle with ourselves. Our negative outlets have been years in the making, but the universe is intelligent and efficient. Once you have a breakthrough in recognition, you will quickly go through a series of changes in circumstances that, while they may seem negative, will always be to your advantage. When you take action to initiate positive change, you are contributing to the evolution of our species.

In becoming a more compassionate person, you are bound to influence someone else to be more compassionate. That person will infect someone else, and it will become a good virus. When you change an old negative pattern, you are affecting yourself at the molecular level by influencing your DNA. Many of the negative traits we carry have also been passed down through our DNA. Our nurture affects our nature and vice versa. I've read how external factors can actually change our DNA by temporarily modifying its sequence. Epigenetics, meaning "attached to the DNA," is the study of such modification. We have been hostage to patterns imprinted in our DNA for too long. It's perfect timing for change and because we are powerful spiritual beings, it can happen for us. When we align ourselves with a higher power, it will move freely through us, empowering us with the divine.

"Life is either a Daring Adventure or it's nothing."

—Helen Keller

Transformation Awaits

It is crucial to invest time into discovering how our hidden emotions and sporadic attitudes dominate us. Finding our life purpose is not only about discovering our dream job; that would not be enough if we were still unsatisfied with our lives. We become satisfied by matching our internal state with our external state—by being real. If we don't change our positions to our viewpoints and responses, we will forever carry reactive behavior, bound to ourselves and others. We must prime ourselves to release old resentments, to clean house and assimilate events in a more powerful and constructive way. If we are coming from reactive behavior, we will never be able to clearly assess our opportunities. All the answers lie within us, and these guides will show us the way.

To change, we will need to transmute our character flaws into character virtues, but first we must identify them. This may be difficult because we don't even know we have them. There are parts of us so deeply conditioned that they're difficult for us to see. However, those closest to us may have called us out on them. In the moment, it will sound like someone is disrespecting us or taking their frustrations out on us, but the truth is that others are just mirrors reflecting back at us who we are showing up as.

Eventually we will catch sight of our flaws, not because we recognize them but because we see their harmful results. The end result of wrong action can never be good. Eventually, we become frustrated and hopefully desperate for change. Life usually administers us a good beating before we want change. However, this is the place where change can best be initiated.

We've already made great progress by admitting our lack of control over our incessant thoughts and coming to believe that our higher power could restore us and help us through this journey. We've also cleaned house by taking a personal inventory on paper, probably for the first time, and we've confessed our wrongs to God, ourselves, and another human being. It is time to take it a step further. We will now identify these character flaws, the ones we've used to navigate through life, and we will transmute them into virtues. You already have a map.

EXERCISE 4: PART A—CHARACTER FLAWS

For this exercise, pull out your inventory list from Exercise 3: Part B on page 54 and take a look at the fourth column. This is the row showing your part in the events. See the list of character flaws on page 67 (I'm sure there are more, but these should be enough for this exercise). Look at all the character flaws and write down all the ones that apply to the actions you took in the fourth column, then write those flaws in the fifth column. Here's my example again:

Who/ What I Am Resenting	The Cause of My Resentment	Affects My…	My Wrongs	Character Flaws
My mom	She didn't let me take singing lessons as a child.	Emotional and societal well-being.	I treated her badly thereafter; I would defy her and became disrespectful.	Selfishness, critical, anger, resentment, hatred
My boyfriend	He's controlling and doesn't let me be me.	Emotional, financial, societal, and sexual well-being.	I mistreated him and belittled him. I was dishonest and cruel.	Selfish, self-seeking, untrustworthy, lack of integrity
My boss	He's unpredictable and inconsiderate.	Financial, emotional, and societal well-being	I was inconsiderate and worked just enough to get by. I tapped into the business account.	Selfishness, dishonesty

Who/ What I Am Resenting	The Cause of My Resentment	Affects My...	My Wrongs	Character Flaws
My brother	He only calls when he needs something.	Emotional and financial well-being.	I only called him when I needed something. I was not honest about how I felt about our relationship.	Critical, negative thinking, untrustworthiness
The government	They overtax us and keep secrets.	Financial and societal well-being.	I became cynical, caused discord instead of harmony, and became alienated.	Judgmental, critical
The Bible	It's extremely negative; I see a punishing God.	Emotional and societal well-being.	I became close-minded and cynical and judged people I considered "Bible thumpers."	Selfish, unreasonable expectations

When you are done, you will come face-to-face with your most glaring character flaws. You may have listed all of them or just repeated a few. You will now see the tools you have been using to navigate through your relationships and through life. Here, you will get to see yourself not for *who you think you are*, but for *who you have been*. You will now possess a clarity few have. Armed with this knowledge, true change can happen for you.

These character flaws can be transmuted, but you must ask your higher power for help. You must turn over all the flaws standing in the way of you and your fellows. Having taken a good, hard look at your faults, with paper in hand, you may want to say a prayer like this:

My Higher Power,

I ask that you take all of me, the good and the bad. I pray that you transmute every character flaw standing in the way of reaching my life purpose. Please transmute every flaw into a virtue so that I better serve all others in my life. Amen.

You must ask your higher power to take them, root and all. When I identified my character flaws, I was appalled at how selfish I'd been throughout my life. I placed unreasonable expectations on everyone. That one in particular was a shocking blow, for it revealed how entitled I'd been. It takes courage to face ourselves. Once we have come face-to-face with our flaws and owned them, we must be willing to release them. To change ourselves, we must replace old behaviors with new ones. You cannot just remove something and create a vacuum; that space must be filled. Next, you will learn how to turn these liabilities into assets.

Character Flaws

- Abusive/hurtful
- Anger/resentment/hatred
- Anxiety
- Arrogance
- Childishness
- Controlling
- Critical/judgmental
- Defiance
- Discontentedness
- Dishonesty
- Emotional sensitivity
- Envy
- Financial irresponsibility
- Gluttony
- Greed/materialism
- Impatience
- Insecurity
- Intolerance
- Irritability
- Jealousy
- Lack of integrity
- Lust
- Martyrdom
- Moodiness
- Negative thinking
- Overdependence
- Perfectionism
- Prone to gossip
- Restlessness
- Sarcasm
- Self-centeredness
- Self-condemnation
- Self-destructiveness
- Self-importance/grandiosity
- Self-justification
- Self-pity
- Self-seeking
- Selfishness
- Sloth/procrastination/laziness
- Sulking/scorn
- Unreasonable expectations
- Unreliability
- Untrustworthiness

We Are Alchemists

> "Everything is Dual; everything has poles; everything has its pair of opposites; like and unlike are the same; opposites are identical in nature, but different in degree; extremes meet; all truths are but half-truths; all paradoxes may be reconciled."
>
> —The Kaolin

Love and hate are identical in nature but different in degrees, as are hot and cold. The energy itself is not removed; it is merely polarized. This is great news because it means that if you are selfish, you have the ability to be generous; if you are unhappy, you can be happy; and if you are anxious, you can be content. The positive quality already exists as a potential within the flaw. Please take a look at the following list. You now have before you a list of character virtues. They are the opposites of the defects you previously identified.

CHARACTER VIRTUES

Abusive/hurtful = gentle, praising, positive, caring

Anger/resentment/hatred = peace, joy, forbearance

Anxiety = calmness, equanimity, tranquility, serenity

Arrogance = humility, modesty

Childishness = mature, experienced, grownup

Controlling = yielding, accepting, pliable

Critical/judgmental = praising, favorable, celebrating, approving

Defiance = obedience, respect, subordination

Discontentedness = satisfied, thankful, fulfilled

Dishonesty = sincerity

Emotional sensitivity = calm, stoic, strong

Envy = goodwill, sympathy, regard

Financial irresponsibility = stable, responsible, timely

Gluttony = moderation, restraint

Greed = generous, temperance

Impatience = calm, patient, peaceful

Insecurity = confident, assured, protected, tranquil

Intolerance = open-minded, fairness, tolerance
Irritability = calm, composed, good-humored, tranquil
Jealousy = confident, appreciative
Lack of integrity = honorableness, virtue, principle, honesty
Lust = calm resistance
Martyrdom = favor, satisfaction, relief, bliss
Moodiness = stable, happiness, cheer, pleasure
Negative thinking = confidence, optimism
Overdependence = independence, self-sufficiency
Perfectionism = easygoing, tolerant, yielding
Prone to gossip = silence, quiet
Restlessness = relaxed, content, composed, peaceful
Sarcasm = compliment, mildness, regard, respect
Self-centeredness = unselfishness, humbleness
Self-condemnation = good conscience, mercifulness
Self-destructiveness = self-realization, self-love, self-appreciation
Self-importance/grandiosity = generosity
Self-justification = self-knowledge
Self-pity = mental strength, hope, self-courage
Self-seeking = selfless, considerate, generous
Selfishness = gracious, kind, altruistic
Sloth/procrastination/laziness = vitality, energy, zeal
Sulking/scorn = praise, respect, honor, tolerance, acceptance
Unreasonable expectations = sensible, reasonable, workable
Unreliability = steady, reliable, secure, faithful
Untrustworthiness = reliable, dependable, faithful, trustworthy

EXERCISE 4: PART B—CHARACTER VIRTUES

For this exercise, you will review your list of character flaws and next to each flaw write down its virtue. If you cannot find the character virtue that corresponds to the character flaw, do a google search for antonyms or look at the list I provided. Here's an example: Selfish = Generous.

Once you have created this list of character virtues, these are the qualities you will begin to practice to replace the old behavior or character flaw. To begin the process, cut little strips of paper. Write one of the virtues you wish to incorporate into your life on each strip. I understand this may sound like a lot of work, and it is, but it is a small price to pay for the amount of change that will be initiated in your life. If you don't go through the action, it will not have the significance or energetic weight for the change to occur. You are inducing change, with your higher power's help always.

Now, grab your HP Box (see page 36). Find a way to put a divider in it so you can keep your fears and troubles you turn over to your Higher Power separate from the virtues you're about to put in. Fold your strips of paper into tiny packages. Make them small enough to fit inside your box. They do not have to be in any particular order. Then place them inside the box. In the morning, choose one and unfold it to see what it is. Focus on practicing that virtue for the rest of the day. You can then put it back in. You may pick up the same one several times and that's okay. Once you feel you have mastered this virtue, you can then throw it away or keep it somewhere else as a memory. I still have my old ones. I keep them only as a memory to help me remember how far I've come.

You are training your brain to break old patterns and ways of thinking. This exercise will help you form new connections and new responses. You must do so to strengthen your new and positive behaviors. You will find many instances throughout the day where you will able to practice the character virtue. Like all new things, at first it might feel uncomfortable, but if you persist, you will soon realize the power you truly possess to initiate change.

Practice replacing one behavior with another. Wishful thinking and hoping alone will not do—you must perform the action. *Faith* is a verb, and you must work it. Continue this exercise every day for about two weeks or at least until you have had a chance to work through all your character flaws and have now replaced them with virtues. It's okay to repeat a few. In fact, I encourage it. You are forming new connections and will strengthen new behaviors. You are priming your brain for a new reality.

Building New Hardware

When we exercise our spiritual muscles, we create new hardware in our brains. Every time we try something new, we strengthen a new behavior. Every time we take a new risk or dream a new dream, our brain receptors are creating new connections, literally rewiring our brains. As we break old patterns and engage in new, healthier behaviors, the old connections will weaken and begin to break down. Normally we are living a record of the past. This is the place where we feel most comfortable because it has been reinforced thousands of times. Old behaviors get burned into our memories and become part of our personalities.

One of our goals should be matching our internal feelings with what we are projecting to the outside world. In the beginning, we will have to "act as if." Our new behaviors will not yet match what we are used to feeling on the inside. This, too, will change—sometimes very quickly. We must do it until it becomes real. It is natural for our new behaviors to seem fake or unnatural. After all, we are pruning old connections. In time, you will gain great pleasure in doing the right thing and then the consequences will speak for themselves. Judge them by their fruits.

> *"A good tree cannot bear bad fruit, nor can a bad tree bear good fruit. Every tree that does not bear good fruit is cut down and thrown into the fire. Therefore by their fruits you will know them."*
>
> —Matthew 7:15-20

So far you have created awareness, which helps you toward ego deflation; placed your dependence on your higher power; and done an inventory and confessed your wrongs. Now you have identified your character flaws and must turn them over to your higher power. You must seek its guidance and strength to transmute these old reactive patterns into character virtues.

Do not be afraid to surrender these aspects of yourself. We may never be saints, but we must be willing to grow along spiritual lines. Always strive toward progress and not perfection. We must do our best given our circumstances and remember there will always be changes happening. Do not be afraid of change; it's the most common event of our lives. Always be grateful, even for your challenges. They are the fuel that initiates greatness within us. Remember, you will not lose your identity through this process; you will only surrender the parts of yourself no longer serving you. Your spirit and your innate gifts can never be dulled. Nothing of value is ever lost through this process; it will simply help your true nature shine through.

6

LETTING GO OF HEAVY STUFF

Spiritual Principles: Human Love and Self-Discipline

"The love we give away is the only love we keep."

—Elbert Hubbard

In working these exercises, hopefully you've come to discover you have been living through reactive patterns. These reactions only serve to perpetuate old systems that bring misery. Now, having identified your character flaws and having replaced them with new behaviors, you are poised to create victorious change. You have been called to do the best you can, and when you do your best, you shall do better and move up the spiritual ladder of evolution.

At this point, you can see there are obvious patterns of damaged relations due to your incessant thinking. Defective relationships are usually the byproduct of dysfunctional thinking. Just because everyone seems to be doing it does not make it okay. Having undergone a personal inventory, you will want to set right any past harms. If you are to be free, a conscious creator, you must be released from the confines of the past.

The exercise in this chapter is about healing personal relations. The spiritual principles called into action here are empathy and human love. To call forth your creative powers, it is best to clear the baggage of the past in the form of toxic thoughts and damaged relations. Looking back, you can see how you may have caused strains in your personal relationships. Many times we've stepped on the toes of our brothers and sisters, and they have retaliated. Life is too short to be spent holding resentment or guilt from your past actions, but it is never too late to make right. You will always have an opportunity to mitigate past damage. You are now working along spiritual lines, which means you do not have to abide by linear time, nor do you have to wait for the law of karma to compensate. You have the free will to mitigate past wrongs, thereby avoiding the backward swing of the pendulum of karma.

But more than anything, you must do this for yourself. You must be released from the bondage of ego, and the next exercise is one of the most liberating of all. Creating the space to right a wrong will be one of the biggest gifts you can give yourself. Your ego will receive a crushing blow. You will be humbled by the grace that will come to you, compelling you to act. At a deep level, human beings are compelled to exercise forgiveness. The world is forgiving to a noble heart.

What Is Karma?

Much has been written about karma. No one really knows if it exists as a fact, but we can still be guided by the laws of cause and effect for great insight. Because we are free to choose, we can choose an action bound to cause a positive or negative reaction or effect. If we choose a negative action, we are likely to receive a negative effect. However, by choosing a positive action, we may be able to transmute a negative effect into something more favorable.

Some people believe we carry karma from our previous lifetimes. Regardless of where our challenges are coming from, we can always correct our behaviors in the here and now to ease the burden of our transgressions. The present moment is our greatest ally, for it holds the key to liberation. Like alchemists, we hold the power to transmute circumstances through our choices and behaviors. We should treat each moment in our lives with great care and attention because each day creates ripple effects compounded through time.

As mentioned, we must learn to forgive others. This is essential if we are to forgive ourselves. You are now at a higher level of awareness than many others on the planet. Most people will not go through the trouble of doing a personal inventory or searching for their character flaws. Being at a higher level of awareness gives you great power, and with great power comes great responsibility. You must now be the "bigger person." While this sounds like a tall order, it will come naturally to you. Doing the next right thing will become spontaneous because you will no longer be dominated by the incessant demands of your mind. You are vibrating on higher ground, and your actions will be guided and intuitive. Remember what was said about forgiveness: We must give it to get it. Most of our reactive patterns are fear-based. Forgiveness releases us from fear, and fear is the biggest obstacle between our higher power and ourselves—the power we are trying to tap into.

The following exercise helps you take any guilt or negativity from the past and allow for freedom and healing. You will now have a chance to be absolved, as far as your spirit is concerned, from your transgressions that mostly live in the memory of your past. Prudence and care are of major importance. We would not want to rehash the past and make matters worse. But if you are honest and come with an open mind and heart, it will not matter what the other person's response is. You will have cleaned up your side of the street and you will be free. How others respond is not your business; your business is to set right any wrongs.

EXERCISE 5: PART A—CREATING A CLEAN SLATE

On a sheet of paper or in your journal, if you have one, make a list of all the people, places, or things from your past you feel you've done harm to. This step is particularly important because it will help you begin to reconstruct a clean slate within your mind. Whether the incident you are holding on to is true or imagined, it lives in your mind. It is taking up the valuable energy you will need to reach higher states of happiness and freedom.

If something has been bothering you for any length of time, write it down. If you have a hard time identifying what might be bothering you, take another look at the fourth column on your inventory list. There you will get a glimpse at some of the harms you've done to others. Maybe some of those people belong on this new list. It will often be close relatives, partners, and friends, but it can also be places, institutions, religions, or the government. It may be something recent or from long ago. The fact you still remember it means it is taking up valuable space in your mind. There is nothing too insignificant to go on this list. If you can remember, it belongs on your list.

I remember an incident that took place very long ago, which I thought was foolish, but it turned out to be a lesson in empathy and care. I was in kindergarten and there was this boy named Edgard, whom I hated for no reason. I couldn't stand the look of his curly hair, and I'd fantasize about being mean to him. I wasn't a cruel kid, but I sure showed signs of cruelty in this instance. One day when the teacher left the class, I had my chance. I ran up to the kid as fast as I could and pulled his curly hair as hard as I possibly could. The boy looked back at me with a saddened but surprised look, and asked me, "But why?" That moment changed me. The amount of empathy and pain I shared with Edgard was beyond my five-year-old mind. I felt so bad and guilty for a long time. I continued to ask myself that same question: "But why?" I still don't know why, and I may never know. Sometimes "why" is not a good question. What I do know is how we are often mean to each other. Sometimes it seems "justified," and other times we are simply carrying our own secret pain.

Throughout my journey, I've come to realize we are often afraid of each other because we have been afraid of our own inadequacies. We must always choose mercy and open our hearts and minds if we are to transform circumstances in our favor. No law can ever be more merciful than the law of forgiveness. At some point in time, we have all been victims and oppressors. I believe we can all benefit from the gentle gift of forgiveness.

EXERCISE 5: PART B—WILLINGNESS TO MAKE AMENDS

After making a list of all the people you have harmed, become willing to make amends to them. The willingness to make amends for past damage has tremendous healing properties. It is a protective balm against karma and will soothe your aching soul. This action must be genuine to reap the benefits. If you are not willing to make amends, if you think you are unable to, or if you lack courage, pray to your higher power and ask for willingness until it comes.

There are times when an actual amends will no longer be possible due to circumstances. The person may have passed away or it may do more harm than good to reach them. You must simply write a list confirming you are *willing* to make an amends. Although it is not possible, the fact you are willing will grant you the desired relief and protection.

Simply writing it down on paper and feeling it in your innermost self is great progress. Once you have written your list, this stagnant energy will begin to lose its grip and you will feel great relief. You are releasing an amends into the universe, and it always listens. It's the beginning of the end of isolation and fear of your fellow brothers and sisters. Once you are done writing your list, take some time to contemplate it.

Break down your list into three sections:

- Amends you can make.
- Amends you might be able to make at a future date.
- Amends you can never make.

Once you have made the divisions, take a contemplative look. What amends can you make now? Who are they? Are they people close to you?

Verify within yourself if it would be helpful to make amends or if it would inflict further damage. Take the time to reflect on each one of them. You never want to make amends to simply make yourself feel better. You are to take the whole into consideration, taking careful measures not to hurt another. Let's say you have withheld a secret from someone over something you did in the past. You must contemplate if it is a good idea to bring up the past or if it is best left alone. You are never to make a direct amends if it will cause further damage to others. Many times the best amends you can make is to leave something alone and never go back there again. If you have engaged in bad behavior, been unfaithful or the sort, you can write it down and promise to your innermost self never to engage in that type of behavior again. If you are honest about your oath, you will be spared.

Still, sometimes we are called to do a living amends because there are things for which we cannot do direct amends. Living amends consist of doing the right thing throughout the remainder of our lives to the best of our abilities. If done from the heart, this earnest desire to set the past straight will grant you absolution for your transgressions, given they are not perpetuated. My living amends to my family is to be present and truthful, for I was an absent parent for a long time. Saying sorry is not enough; we must take definite action aimed directly at correcting a transgression. Sometimes it is best to have a heart-to-heart talk, which means an open and honest dialogue with no hidden agenda other than seeking an honest acknowledgment on your part.

Then there are financial amends. You may owe someone money. It will cost you more in spiritual energy to never try to correct this. You can simply tell your creditor you are willing to make things right and explain to them what terms are realistic for you. If you are not ready to do this, commit to making this a priority when the right moment comes.

If one of the amends on your list has legal implications, pray for guidance. Your higher power would not want to put you in a position where you could not be of service to others. Perhaps you will be guided to get legal advice. This is a gentle yet profound process. My suggestion is to get advice from a professional, but take some type of action, even if it means just writing it down and praying about it. The fact you are willing to make amends means your answers are on the way.

It's not about trying to be right or justifying yourself. You are here to undo damage you may have caused. You should ask, "Is there any way I can make it right?" Many times you will find most people will be satisfied knowing you've stepped up. It does not matter if the person accepts or does not accept your position; you are here to clean your side of the street. Even though the person does not accept your approach, your mission will have been fulfilled, for you have done everything within your personal power to correct a situation.

There are times when the moment is not right to make amends due to distance or circumstance. You cannot shy away from perpetually not taking this step on that account. You can write out how you are willing in the future to make this amends and write out a few ways you could approach the situation. When the moment is right, you will then be ready to move forward. In the meantime, if you are honest, you will reap the benefit of absolution.

Then there will be the people to whom you can never make personal amends, although you can always make living amends. Although the person may have passed, you can still take several actions. One thing you can do is write a letter stating how you feel and how you would have made your amends if you could. You can then perform a little ritual and maybe burn the letter in a fireplace or at the beach. Or you can write a letter and keep it, or you can take up a cause in memory of the person. You can also do a living amends by committing to having learned from your experience and becoming a better person by it in honor to them.

I can never make amends to Edgard, unless he happens to read this and can still remember what happened, but I have made it a living amends to be a compassionate and caring person filled with empathy. I've found inner love, and this has caused me to love others at a deeper level. This is my amends to Edgard. I had many others on my list of amends, including the IRS, banks, and family members. There were some that seemed impossible, but a little at a time, I was guided in how to approach each one in a loving and gentle way.

It really helps to have a great friend, mentor, or spiritual advisor to help you on this step. You might want to work with the person who helped you with the admission of your wrongs. A detached person will always have broader perspectives. Let them know what you're doing. Once you know how you will tackle each one, get a second opinion. A second opinion from a trusted source is invaluable.

Defeating "Evil"

As I mentioned, like alchemists, we have the power to transmute circumstances by the choices we make. We must learn to understand the nature of evil. Evil is a stepping-stone toward growth; the amount of pain we cause ourselves and others is up to us. Evil or wrong thoughts must be understood. We must come to realize it is a passing phase of the human experience. All evil or wrong thinking is a misunderstanding in perception, therefore it can only be temporary. What seems to be an evil or bad event is simply a life lesson being revealed. Many times, what seems to be a painful event turns out to be a future blessing in disguise. Still, there will be things we cannot make sense of. There are lessons we will eventually understand through the passage of time. In the meantime, we must learn to find acceptance.

There is no evil in our present awareness—that is, as things are taking place. Evil is only a name we assign to a past event, which we were not present enough to understand at the time. We must then strive to become more conscious in present state awareness, the place where we can always rise to the occasion and where any state whatsoever can be met.

As long as we ignore the unpleasant circumstances that keep recurring in our lives, we will be subject to evil. But by guarding our minds and checking in with our higher selves, we will always be provided the tools to defeat it. Life will happen; pain is mandatory, but suffering is optional. If you choose to flood your mind with negativity and resentments, one day they will manifest as your own creations. As human beings, we seem to manifest both what we love most and what we fear most. Once we can understand there is nothing to fear, healing will occur quite rapidly.

Flood your mind with positive thoughts, make faith your ally, and trust in your higher self. Pay attention to your thoughts—many are useless, but some are clues. Be the observer of your thoughts rather than the monkey mind thinking the thoughts. Remember, thoughts are like passing clouds, but you are the sky. Learn to spend time in reflection and meditation. If you continue having recurring thoughts that won't go away, take a look at them and befriend them; they are speaking to you.

These exercises will work, but there are times when you may need professional help. Do not be afraid to ask for help. I am not a professional; I am simply a guide coaching you through life lessons that have helped me, and I am confident they can help you, too. Finding a mentor or a spiritual advisor is also especially important. You will always receive guidance if you ask. Every obstacle you face in life is a lesson in need of conquering. Fear will lose its grip one lesson at a time. Use pain as an indicator to push your limits and force yourself to respond to life events. Learn to embrace pain and know there lies a valuable lesson within it. All your choices, conscious and subconscious, have gotten you where you are today. Keep what serves you and discard the rest. Part of finding your life purpose is conquering your fears. Make peace with every moment; it is a lesson that reveals you to yourself.

7
USING THE SPACE TO CREATE

Spiritual Principles: Perseverance and Spirituality

"The spiritual life does not remove us from the world but leads us deeper into it."

—Henri J. M. Nouwen

You have now prepared yourself to embark on a great adventure. You have taken important steps by clearing heavy energies from your past, and now there is room to create. By doing the exercises in the previous chapters, you have chosen to partake in the evolution of your spirit. Congratulations. Many people die without ever questioning why they do the things they do. Most of us have to pay the price of suffering before we ever come close to taking such rigorous action, but the price has been well worth it. You will now gain a new sense of joy and freedom, which would not have been possible had you not been beaten into submission by life.

With this new canvas before you, what will you want next? Choosing to participate in the evolution of your spirit shall now become a way of life. You are to guard this new freedom from the rust of idleness. You must continue to stretch your spiritual muscles daily. Each day you should incorporate some type of practice to enhance your inner world. You must hunger to be closer and closer to your source, the place where your inexhaustible well of strength lies. You must be vigilant of your actions. Your self-awareness must increase or else you may slide back into old habits.

Throughout our days, we have thousands of thoughts and take hundreds of actions. It is difficult to keep track of all our daily actions even though we are now much more conscious. If we are to persevere, keeping our temple clean should be our way of life.

So far, you may have chosen to do the previous exercises on separate sheets of paper. That's okay, but if you don't have a journal yet, I encourage you to get one for the upcoming exercise. Even if you aren't accustomed to journaling, I ask that for sake of this journey, you give it a chance. Journaling will serve as an early warning system to show you what direction you are moving in before you find yourself back in the middle of your old ways. It is a safeguard against your old habits and a great tool of awareness. It will reveal who you are showing up as in life.

You will be journaling your answers to four questions each night before you go to sleep. There are no right or wrong answers to the questions; they are here to reveal you to yourself. You can do this any time during the day, but I suggest you do it at night because it has given me the best results. It works better than taking a sleeping pill because it will empty your psyche of the day's worries or concerns. In turn, it will reduce the buildup of stagnant energy in your mind and body.

Clearing away negative energy will help you hear the voice within. You will become in tune to hunches through intuitive hints or someone's words. Your subconscious mind will always make decisions way before your conscious mind is aware. This means whatever is in your subconscious will direct you. You should learn to take time to check in with yourself before entering your dream state. For six to eight hours, you will be immersed in the world of your subconscious. It is always trying to make sense of things and trying to make life easier; you simply do not understand it.

We can collaborate with our subconscious minds by helping facilitate the creative process it is trying to achieve. By making a habit of clearing our minds before we go to bed, we give our minds a clean slate from all our daily trouble. The goal is to become more aware and learn to use this wonderful tool. In doing a nightly inventory, we will learn to recognize the things we are impressing in our minds. The type of information we allow inside us will become important to us. Every time we think, we activate the potential to influence our subconscious. This is where our operating system lies and where true change can take place. We now have better access to this software because we've taken important steps in clearing the programs that were keeping us stuck. Now, we must learn to guard and nurture it. We must tend it like a garden, allowing the sunlight of the spirit to shine freely.

As we exercise our spiritual muscles, we will create new hardware in our brain. Each time we try something new, take a new risk, or dream a new dream, our brain receptors are creating new connections, thereby rewiring our brains. As we begin to strengthen new behaviors, the old connections will become weak and start to break down. Brain cells that fire together wire together. The knowledge and application of this discovery grants you great power.

EXERCISE 6: NIGHTLY INVENTORY

The spiritual principle behind this step is perseverance. This exercise helps you come closer to your true nature. It's like a deep scrub to remove all impurities so the truth may shine forth. In your journal, respond to the following questions:

1. Did I become angry today?
2. When did I behave better than I wanted to?
3. What did I notice about life that made me feel happy to be alive?
4. What did I do for someone else today?

Before I did this exercise, I wasn't in the habit of going back and reviewing my day. Trying to remember felt exhausting. When I was first instructed to incorporate these questions into my nightly routine, the idea seemed random, but I soon learned its value. To give you an idea of how these questions can help, here is a rundown of each question and its purpose:

1. DID I BECOME ANGRY TODAY?

Analyzing whether or not you became angry over the course of the day offers you an opportunity for introspection. This probably isn't something you normally give much thought to. This question will trigger a succession of memories, and you will be forced to recall and be honest with yourself about any anger you felt. You may or may not have acted out in anger, but if you did, you must have felt it. This exercise helps you stay true to yourself and become more aware of the present moment. While this is a simple yes-or-no question, answering it allows you to observe your emotional and mental responses. You can choose to stop right there or take it a step further, as I usually do, and write more details about each experience of anger to fully answer the question. This is not a test; it is simply an exercise in revelation. Above all, we must continue to be truthful to ourselves if we are to grow in spiritual awareness.

This exercise will reveal whether you owe someone an apology. You've already worked on an important exercise in the previous chapter: You made a list of people you'd harmed through the years. In doing this nightly inventory, you will have a chance to recognize on a daily basis whether you've acted wrongly and respond promptly. When we are wrong, we must learn to promptly admit it. This will prevent us from having to go through the trouble of making future amends. When things are addressed promptly, many problems can be avoided. If you notice your bad conduct as it happens, mitigate it quickly. The sooner the better, before it has a chance to sink into your subconscious.

2. WHEN DID I BEHAVE BETTER THAN I WANTED TO?

This question demands even more awareness This is an odd question, because we do not usually behave better than we want to. This question challenges you to have greater discipline in your everyday responses. An example of behaving better than you want to might simply be not hanging up the phone without saying goodbye or practicing restraint on taking any action that would make you unhappy in the end. We can sometimes get instant gratification by cutting someone off while they are speaking to us because we don't want to hear what they are saying or may think we know what they are going to say. By exercising restraint, we may not get instant gratification (on the contrary, it may be grueling), but we will have practiced one of life's valuable tools, the practice of self-discipline.

Perhaps you don't usually behave better than you want to. Answering this question will compel you to take a different action than you are used to. People who are present in awareness will not behave poorly. When we do, we've lost presence and are reacting based on our character flaws. Perhaps you are conscious and tend to respond better than you feel. You may have self-restraint and more awareness than the average person. Maybe you normally respond better than you want to with strangers. Family members and friends may be more challenging. By answering this question, you will bring even more awareness into your life. There are nights when my answer to this question is "Today, I behaved exactly the way I felt." This is a wonderful place to be because it reveals that my internal states are congruent with my external actions. I am in perfect flow.

3. WHAT DID I NOTICE ABOUT LIFE THAT MADE ME GRATEFUL TO BE ALIVE?

This question helps you see more clearly what often gets contaminated by the dramas in our lives. In becoming aware of this question, you are forced once again into the present moment. You are reminded to realize there are many things to be grateful for. It doesn't have to be a big thing. You might simply notice someone's smile as you are walking down the street. You might hear a child's laughter or the sound of leaves rustling in the breeze. You can be grateful for the people in your life and for the ones who have departed. You can be grateful for the visible things in your life, but you can also be grateful for the things that are on their way. When you take the time to recognize the things that make you glad, you are sending off a vibration of gratitude into the universe, and the universe will always respond. The more you are able to be thankful for, the greater your joy. A grateful heart is the antidote to sorrow and depression. You must make it a habit to notice the good in your life instead of giving so much power to the negative events.

4. What did I do for someone else today?

This question opens your awareness to your inner desire to give back to life. At a deep level, most of us yearn to make a contribution. By carrying this subconscious message in your mind, you will be prompted to carry out random acts of kindness wherever possible. You may already do this practice as a way of life, but by acknowledging what you are doing and taking note of it in your heart, you will have greater satisfaction. This is not intended as a way to take credit or receive recognition for your actions, rather it is an inner recognition and an appreciation for the fact that you have the resources available to help another.

The fact you are in a position to help someone else says you have something to give away. You are overabundant in an area where someone else may be lacking. You are reminding yourself of your abundance. In addition, you will have expressed compassion toward your fellow human brothers and sisters. This does not have to be something extreme; it can simply be pausing to let someone pull their car into traffic ahead of you, holding the door for someone, or even just offering a friendly smile. There is no reason we should not do something kind for someone every day. We must learn to inconvenience ourselves to positively affect the life of another.

There are many paths leading to one destination. This is just one of those paths, but it's a path I can attest to. I first had to remove chunks of negative beliefs that had lodged themselves in my body and mind. Through this releasing process, you will come into clear contact with your true self. Once you are closer to your true essence, you will be in closer contact with your true desires and aspirations. When fear, anger, and resentment are no longer taking up our valuable energy, we can show up as the magnificent creators we are.

Prayer and Meditation

> *"Between stimulus and response there is a space. In that space lies our freedom and power to choose our response. In those choices lie our growth and our happiness."*
>
> —Stephen Covey

Congratulations on getting this far! You have done some profound work. By now you should feel a sense of joy and freedom. This is the byproduct of a peaceful mind. You have created a higher power of your own understanding, cleaned house, and surrendered your character flaws. You've confessed your wrongs and made amends. You have maintained a peaceful state by doing a nightly inventory.

If you have done the exercises to the best of your ability, you may never have to do them again—unless you want to, and that's fine, too. I encourage you to bring these spiritual principles to others in your life. This is what the world needs most. In life, there will always be an ebb and flow, but you never have to stay in a dark place for long. These final thee exercises are recommended as a practice for daily living.

In addition to taking a nightly inventory, I highly recommend integrating prayer and meditation into your life. You have cleansed yourself of all the heaviness accumulated from the past, but it's like taking a shower. It must become a daily practice for consistent balance. Trust me when I say the time spent on these activities will pay great dividends. Besides your basic necessities, prayer and meditation may be two of the most important activities you do. To sustain your body, you need air, water, and food. To sustain your spirit, prayer and meditation are just as important.

With the hustle and bustle of life, it is easy to lose touch with the most important aspect of our multidimensional selves, our spirit. You can call it consciousness, the subconscious, the energetic body, and many other names, but it is your deeper self. It is the self that makes everything else possible in your outside world. We are so distracted by the external world we lose sight of our inner world, the side of us that although invisible is the most real. Prayer and meditation will help you connect with this subtle aspect of yourself. Once you try them, you will reap the benefits very quickly. Your mind will quiet and you will receive intuitive impulses like never before. You will become present and more aware. You will find peace and create a strong bond with your higher power. You will suddenly get answers to questions that used to baffle you. You will find your higher power will do for you what you could not do through your egoic mind. Meditation will create a space between your thoughts. There will be silence and your answers will come.

While many have practiced prayer and meditation for thousands of years, such practices remain deeply personal. There are many ways to practice prayer and meditation, so choose an individualized version that best suits you. The beauty of spirituality is that unlike organized religion, there are no set rituals to follow. All you need is an honest desire to connect to your higher power. Because you have the freedom to choose the God of your own understanding, you also have the choice to pray or communicate with this force as you please.

Prayer

Prayer is a soft place where the ego becomes humbled. It is one of the most important tools we can use to free ourselves from our ego. We must learn to be present in the here and now, for therein lies our freedom. When we pray, we are opening a channel through which divine guidance can flow. We are acknowledging we don't have all the answers, and this invites humility. We have created a clear channel for divine guidance. We may not get an answer immediately, but the answers *will* come.

When praying, it is tempting to pray for things as we want them to be. That's fine because you are practicing humility and strengthening your connection to your higher power. However, if you learn to pray for divine guidance, the knowledge of its will for you, and the power to carry it out, you will open yourself to receive the most efficient directions of all. As humans, our vision is very limited. We can only see things we've lived, observed, or imagined. Our higher power, on the other hand, has a grander vision than we could ever imagine. Many times, it will brings us much more happiness and fulfillment than we could have ever imagined on our own. This type of trust is built one moment at a time. We must learn to exercise faith as a muscle. Our spiritual muscles are becoming stronger each day.

Faith is trusting that an outcome will turn out for our greater good even though you cannot yet see the final results. Humans have trouble with this because we want guarantees. Faith is hopeful expectation between outcomes without cynicism. It also comes from realizing many times we're not happy to get what we thought we wanted, but everything we've ever received has prepared us for our next step. Everything adds value to our life, especially the difficult lessons. Learning to trust the process takes practice in faith. We must make prayer a daily practice to improve our conscious contact with our higher power.

EXERCISE 7: MORNING PRAYER

In the first part of this exercise, I ask you to start your day with a prayer. If you aren't used to praying, this process may at first feel unnatural, but, as with other steps on this journey, you must continue to do it until it becomes real. Simply begin a dialogue with your awesome higher power. It can be in the form of a simple conversation. Your mission is to fine-tune your allegiance with your higher power. The way we form human bonds is through communication. Although our higher power knows even more about us than we now about ourselves, we may not really believe it. It is our job to approach our source and forge this truest of bonds. This type of bond will give us faith beyond our human reach; it will always be here for us. There is no human power that can ever come close to the unity we will feel once we have reached this level of communication.

Through the years, I have formed my own ritual in the mornings. For me, it's kneeling before I state my prayers. Kneeling works for me because it forces me to take an action of humility and brings me into awareness. I remember the first time I tried kneeling—how awkward it felt, but it forced me to communicate more honestly; it made me more present. Everything you can do to make you present will serve you well. I realized that first time when I kneeled how disconnected I was from my source. I had always prayed while lying on my back half asleep (when I remembered), but through kneeling, there was this energetic connection where I felt in the presence of a power greater than myself. My ego was humbled. Always find a position that feels best to you.

You can begin slowly, but you must bring awareness to the act of praying. Ask for guidance and thank this power for all the blessings in your life. Prayers of gratitude are the best. This is a recognition of all that is good in your life. When we pray in the spirit of gratitude, more good things keep coming. We have so many things to be grateful for, yet we often carelessly overlook them. You can also set an intention for the day and ask your higher power to help you carry it out. Ask it to guide you toward your life purpose. The answers will come, but not necessarily within your desired timeframe. You don't know the perfect combination needed to prepare you for your highest purpose, but your higher power does.

Throughout the rest of the day, listen for messages and begin to notice synchronicities. Because you are now more present and aware, you will hear the messages more clearly. Messages come in many forms. Do not dismiss anything as a coincidence. Listen with all your senses but especially with your heart. What used to be an occasional hunch will become a working part of your mind.

"The typical wildflower whom many carelessly trample, in the eyes of the poet, a message from the heavens."

—James Allen

MEDITATION

There are as many ways to meditate as there are people roaming this earth. There are guided meditations and silent meditations. There are many apps you can download for a plethora of choices. The smartphone app Insight Timer, for example, has many free meditations you can listen to. Whatever meditation you choose, the point of meditation is to quiet your mind long enough to receive messages from your higher power.

Your higher power is within you and speaks, but you may have chosen to forget and ignore this subtle vibration. Because the mind is incessantly thinking, it's not likely you will begin to clearly notice guidance right away. At first, it will be subtle. Meditation takes practice and must become a way of life to keep experiencing its benefits. You will always be making a forward movement when you meditate, even if you don't feel it right away. Slowly you will begin to learn how to still your mind. This is great progress; all you have to bring is your willingness.

Early in my meditation days, I began to notice how people who meditated had an attractive peace about them. Their eyes seemed to shine brighter, and their words carried more wisdom. Something profound was happening to this group that was not happening to those who didn't meditate. This quality of peace and deep wisdom was very attractive to me, and it encouraged me to keep meditating. I asked many questions of meditators and meditation teachers, and I got many answers, but the one thing all the answers shared in common was that I had to make meditation a *daily* practice.

Meditation is not something to practice once in a while. Even if it's just for five minutes a day, you must make it a daily practice. In time, you will begin to look forward to meditation because it will break the mental time-space continuum and you will tap into present-moment awareness. The time you meditate will grow longer. I recommend you meditate in the morning before you start your day. Even if it means getting up twenty minutes earlier, it will go a long way. Whenever you choose to meditate, be sure to do it every day for at least five minutes, but ten minutes is an ideal start. I encourage you to ultimately aim for thirty minutes.

Meditation is a reprieve from your incessant thoughts. The ultimate goal in meditation is to be free of thought, but thoughts will always linger. Learn to see them as passing clouds. The thoughts are just clouds and you are the sky.

In the beginning, the thought of having a single focus during meditation was frustrating for me. Then I met Rex, who embodied a spirit of peace, love, and patience. I was grateful he had come to offer a talk on the subject of meditation at a gathering I was attending. He was there to share his meditation experience and guide us through a meditation. He urged us to begin meditating regularly as soon as possible and told us of the benefits it would provide. He then gave us a set of instructions that catapulted me into my current relationship with meditation. I wish to relay his instructions in the following exercise. I am sure it will help you tremendously, as it has helped me. Meditation is now one of the highlights of my life.

EXERCISE 8: COUNTDOWN MEDITATION

Always start your meditation practice by creating conditions in which you feel comfortable and safe. Get cozy. Dim the light or close the shades, and be sure to silence any electronic devices that may disturb you.

For this countdown meditation, take three deep breaths (taking three deep breaths before any meditation practice will help you relax and ground yourself). Breathe in through your nose and carry that breath all the way to your belly. Hold it for five seconds, and then release the breath through your mouth. After you have taken three deep breaths, begin counting backward from 100 to 1 while you envision the number in your mind

This is a simple way to keep your mind focused. When I did this meditation for the first time, I realized that by the time I got to 64, I was lost in thought. I could not reach the number 1 without my thoughts grabbing my attention. At first it was frustrating, and then I began to notice how easily I would lose my concentration. This made me angry at first, but then I later discovered becoming angry would only make it worse. So I began to watch my thoughts and then gently bring myself back to the countdown. At first I had to cut the countdown from 100 to starting at 50 in order to reach 1 in one session. Then gradually I began to gain more control of my mind. It was great insight to realize how fickle-minded I truly was. With practice, I was able to stay focused on the countdown for longer periods, and now, while I am still a spontaneous person, my thoughts are far from fickle.

This countdown meditation is a great introduction to meditation. If you wish, you can base your whole meditation session on taking deep breaths. Simply inhale through your nose and exhale through your mouth, deeply and steadily. There's no need to count, but if you choose to, you can also count your breaths. I encourage you to try many different types of meditations until you discover the one that best fits you.

THE BENEFITS OF MEDITATION

Meditation will not change your essence; it will only enhance your performance and your sense of awareness. It will help you make better decisions. You will come to view your mind as a marvelous tool standing by to help, but you must learn how it operates. It is you who are the operator of your mind, but it's likely that, for the most part, your mind has been using you. Once you learn to sit still during a meditation session, your desire to continue to meditate will grow and your sessions will get longer.

Most important, meditation will improve your conscious contact with your higher power and bring you into your *now* moment. Your mind will become still and you will hear your higher power's guidance. Meditation is your direct path to your higher self. It will guide you toward your heart's desires.

As soon as you start, you will begin to reap the benefits of feeling more peaceful and relaxed. You will notice you have more energy as you go about your day. People and situations will not tire you as easily, for you will be harnessing deep spiritual renewal each day. Your mind will not take you hostage so easily, and you will begin to recognize your conscious awareness versus your egoic mind. Your mind will rest and your body will thank you. This is one of the most important gifts you can ever give yourself.

In time, the practice of meditation will filter into your spirit, and it will be as indispensable as eating and sleeping. The present moment is your gateway to freedom, and you must learn to stay here more often each day. By meditating, your mind will become still and you will be able to visit the present moment more readily. You will realize how the present is not a hostile place, but a place of great freedom, love, and peace. Nothing of value is ever lost in the present moment. It's where we can feel our deepest gratitude and create our biggest healing. It's the place where the peace that surpasses all understanding lives.

Your Thoughts Are Clouds

One of the simplest ways to meditate is to simply watch your thoughts float by. Your thoughts have a short shelf life. When you become present enough to watch them float by like clouds, you will realize you are not your thoughts, that there is a greater intelligence observing all these thoughts floating by. If you were your thoughts, you could not observe them.

The fact you are able to look at them will help you notice there is a greater intelligence at play. Confirm yourself as this greater intelligence and merge with it. This is your true self. This discovery will bring you great peace.

Your mind-identified self will come back with a torrent of attacks and try to pull you from the present, but notice how this can be watched, too. Make this your practice, for herein lies your liberation. Learn to simply watch your thoughts. This sound overly simplistic, but its effects are profound. You will know the difference between an original thought and your ego's because your ego always has a personal interest. Your true self brings you awareness and peace. This place may be foreign at first, but it will quickly become your most desired state. It is your natural state, your true "I am." This is who you are: pure awareness connected to your higher power—not your guilt, your thoughts, or your worries.

Your Mind, Your Ally

It should be everyone's priority to make their minds their ally; the mind is a divine tool and part of consciousness. We must always communicate through honest desire that comes from our hearts. The highest form of asking or prayer comes in the form of thanking. There are many things every day for which we can be thankful. Making a daily gratitude list is a great way to get into the vibration of gratitude. When we are grateful, we are here now. Notice how all of the wonderful perfumes of our spirit come when we are present. We feel gratitude, love, and compassion all in the now moment. Everything happens in the now. Only worry and doubt live in the future or the past.

The most important effect of prayer and meditation is improving your conscious contact with your higher power. Mental concentration is necessary for worldly success; prayer and meditation are necessary for spiritual success. Most of us have practiced prayer in the face of an emergency, but making this a clear line of daily communication is essential to spiritual growth. You might wonder why prayer is necessary if your higher power already knows your heart's desires, and the reason is because we are powerful creators. We have conditioned ourselves to live in fear and doubt and must learn to become present to the now moment where our divine force answers all our prayers. When we are present and still, we are many times more effective at transmitting and receiving our desires. All the power of the universe is backing us, but we must stop the hemorrhage of valuable energy spent on fear and doubt.

The fact we are making a conscious effort to improve our conscious contact with our source makes it many times more powerful. Any action we take consciously will always yield more fruit than an action done haphazardly. This is the power that creates worlds. It is waiting for us to join in on the power of creation. We are to be active participants in the evolution of the universe.

We all want to discover our life purpose. We are all here as co-creators meant to thrive. All our troubles have been here to prepare us on our journey. We can choose to work with this energy that creates worlds to guide us toward our higher good.

We all have a special gift to give this world—*you* are the gift you can give. There is nothing left to do but bring forward your deepest desires. These will always be in harmony with your essence. There is only one of you, and this is your superpower. Without all the rubbish of the past weighing you down, you can now allow your authentic self to shine. Your higher power will always provide everything you need. It is your job to move forward in willingness and desire by becoming present.

YOUR TRUE POWER

Opening this line of communication with your higher power will serve you well in Good Orderly Direction. It will guide you toward your life purpose. You will begin to receive glimpses and intuitive answers to questions that used to puzzle you. Then one action will lead to the next. It is your job to harness the belief that an insight is true for you and never write it off, for insights are whispers of your innermost desires. As a clear channel, you will receive the answers you need to move forward in joy.

8

CONTINUING THE JOURNEY

Spiritual Principle: Service

*"Lord, make me an instrument of your peace...
For it is in giving that we receive;
It is in pardoning that we are pardoned;
And it is in dying that we are born to eternal life."*

—Saint Francis of Assisi

Throughout my journey, I've found I am most fulfilled when I am working in service of others. There seems to be a universal joy expressed when we help others. It has been my observation that we thrive when we are selfless. When I say *service*, I am not referring to direct customer service or a service-oriented position, but rather in the service of helpful contribution to others. Taking the time to care deeply about becoming a better version of yourself bears witness to the fact you will be in a better position to help others. In a sense, we are always in service because people are always observing us. We must learn to lead by example. People will notice the difference between someone being a conscious, caring human and someone who's not. The more we become conscious beings, the more we will be of maximum service to others.

Almost every career or job is linked to "service" in one form to another—from being a lawyer to a plumber to an entertainer. Even jobs based on production are ultimately a service. It is not *what* we do, but *how* we do it. Throughout our days, we get many opportunities to influence each other—the way we show up at work, the way we behave in traffic, or the way we treat a difficult client. These are all opportunities to be of service by showing up as a conscious and evolving human being showing mercy, love, and compassion. Now that we *know* better, we must *do* better and practice these spiritual principles in all our affairs.

We are here to express our deepest desires. Everyone desires health, love, happiness, and financial abundance. In reality, what we are all after is freedom from the bondage of self. We are each a unique expression of life revealing itself to the world. Regardless of the route we choose, we are all worthy, powerful creators. Even if you compare a person who is living a miserable life to someone who is in alignment with their life purpose, you still cannot say one life is more precious than the other. We are all sacred, loving intelligence, but it is up to us *how* we choose to spend our time here.

Regardless of the choices we make, we cannot fail; we are already part of creation. There is nothing you can do that can't be amended. It is up to you to believe this is true. You can come to believe this by watching people who have done it before you. Living your life by the principles in this book, which are timeless, *will* bring you closer to living a fulfilled life and one in which you can be of maximum service to others. There are endless testimonies to this truth.

The purpose of all the exercises you have done so far was to get you in harmony with spiritual principles to guide you throughout your journey. They are meant to clear away the past, which lived in your mind as an illusion. The housecleaning convinced you of how you can now be clear and present as a conscious participant in your life. But its real purpose was to help bring you to your now moment. Nothing exists now but your pure essence, your true nature. Everything else is a result of conditioning. When you practice present-moment awareness, your attention will become razor sharp and you will begin to make intuitive decisions. You will be in perfect alignment with your higher power and you will receive all the assistance you need.

The Magnifying Glass

If we hold a magnifying glass to a piece of paper long enough to focus a ray of sun, the paper will eventually catch fire. Our minds work in the same way. What we focus on expands. The problem is when we fail to focus on the things we want long enough for them to manifest. We must learn to focus on one thing, bring it to fruition, and then create the next. Otherwise, we are creating by default.

Learning to control your thoughts by becoming present is your life's purpose, for it will bring you all you desire. If we learn to focus all our intention on one project at a time, we will have accomplished many projects throughout our life. Life will always get busy with kids, work, and school, but if we are to create something extraordinary, we must discover our calling is to be present now. Life will always give us a second chance, but rarely in the same way. When our expectations are set in stone, we are bound to miss opportunities. By practicing these exercises, we will not tire so easily, for we are now working with infinite intelligence which knows all.

Life is forgiving and resilient, as are you. We must have faith in the process and know the moment will come when we are in alignment with our calling and then we will see. It is a beautiful unfolding. Meditation creates a space between our thoughts. In this silence lie our answers. Our brain will begin to forge new connections and remodel our old dreams. Translating intuitive hints will become your norm. There is a power inside us that will guide us if we let it. It is time to look inside, and meditation is the key.

EXERCISE 9: PART A—WHAT DO YOU ENJOY?

On a blank piece of paper or in your journal, list five things you enjoy doing. They should be things you enjoy so much you would do them for free. For now, simply be aware of them. Then, during your morning prayer and daily meditation, ask your higher power for guidance in finding your life purpose and setting you on the path. For example, "Higher power, please reveal my life purpose to me and lead me in that direction. Please send me clues."

Once you have asked, let it go. Do not fixate on an answer and do not make this the sole focus of your meditation or prayer. Once you have asked, your part is done. Your source will get it at once. If you make the mistake of fixating on this request, you will only create more distance. Ask and release. The answers *will* come. Your higher power communicates in subtle ways. You may not get a direct answer, but you must listen for clues and hunches throughout your day. To do so, you must be present. Practice present-moment awareness as part of your meditation and throughout the day by being the observer of your thoughts. Do not get tangled up with them; remember, they are mostly lies. The intuitive information you need to know will become a spontaneous knowing.

Making this list of five things is a wonderful starting point toward guiding yourself to your inner calling. One or a combination of the activities you listed are likely to be directly connected to your calling, your life purpose. Because you enjoy them, you are bound to be enthusiastic about them. It is likely your passion will develop into a new career path (if that's what you truly desire), but for the time being, start where you are.

EXERCISE 9: PART B—YOUR DEEPEST JOY

Go to a quiet place where you can be by yourself for a few moments and bring sheet of paper or your journal with you. Take a few deep breaths and close your eyes. Try to bring up memories of the thing you loved to do the most in your whole life. Don't worry about how realistic it seems at this point in your life, it's not about that. It's about reliving the moment of joy and passion you used to feel when dreaming about or engaging that activity. Take your time brining back these feelings and savor them. Next, in your journal write down the questions:

1-What feelings did the thought of that activity bring up inside me?

For me it was singing. The feelings it brought up were joy, passion, freedom of expression, happiness, and aliveness.

2-What was it about _____ that evoked such powerful feelings inside me?

For me it was how I felt I was good at it so it evoked confidence, security, and connection. I felt passion as I was singing. It allowed me to express joy, sadness, passion—all those feelings just through the vibration of my voice. It made me happy to believe I was brining joy to the people listening and helping them feel all the feelings I was feeling in the moment.

3-If there was something I could do during the day that could evoke such joy, what would it be?

When I practiced this exercise, I realized how I am able to evoke those same feelings when I am writing or sharing my experience with others. I get the same rush of enthusiasm as I when singing in front of an audience. I can also take singing lessons and re-open this avenue of expression in my life.

I found my gift to be the gift of enthusiasm and passion. Whenever I am exercising this side of myself I am in my highest joy.

If your answer is not coming to you in this moment, don't worry because it will come. You've triggered the feeling of your happiest state so it's been activated, it will take form. I cannot tell you what form it will take because this is very individual, but if you continue to search your answers will come. Remember, your passion does not necessarily have to be your career, but the universe will make a way to merge the two if it is your soul's desire. You can find a pathway for the release of your soul purpose as a hobby while the perfect combination line up. Clarity may come in one fell swoop or in increments.

Now that you are free from the baggage of your past, you will enjoy the present moment in unexpected ways. You may find your current place of work is less unbearable and new opportunities within your current space will open up. You will become free from the bondage of ego and the world will open up to you. It isn't recommended you quit your job and follow your passion all at once unless it's the obvious choice to make. Sometimes acting hastily may bring more trouble as we all have bills to pay and other responsibilities.

However, even if you have the resources to drop what you are currently doing, it is best to let change develop naturally by attracting the right combinations. Once you have felt the freedom of becoming present and unhooked from the past and future, you will have gained freedom. Confirm you are free from the torments of your mind. Remember, what you believe, you magnify.

Find Your Like-Minded Tribe

If you are passionate about something but think you are not good at it, you can always get better. Your passion and enthusiasm will pave the way. Dare to surround yourself with like-minded people. There are always like-minded people, no matter what your form of expression may be, such as sports, science, parenting, gardening, shopping, and more. It is life force expressing itself through creative outlets. If you enjoy art, take an art class. If you like singing, take lessons. Whatever you do, staying present should be your highest purpose. Within this blank canvas lies all the answers, and you are to create them.

Like-minded people are always excited to find each other because we've been there and understand the struggle. For instance, I never believed I could write a book (well, my inner self knew I could, but I didn't). Once I began to practice these exercises, my passion for writing and expressing myself was revealed. The time I had previously spent on blaming the world and feeling sorry for myself was suddenly freed up. I took creative writing classes and read many books. I always made a little time to engage my passion. When attending the creative writing seminars, I always had fun. There were people who acted as mirrors in a hundred forms. The shy one, the one who thinks she can't do it, the one who dares, the professional one—all bound through the passion for expression.

We are always drawn to the things that bring us joy, but never forget your highest joy will come from being present. Once we begin the momentum of joy produced by becoming still and following our passions, opportunities will present themselves. Life will take on new meaning and we will no longer be obsessed by other people or situations. We will have a reprieve from the hustle and bustle of life to follow our hearts. Life is too short not to do so.

There are vast arenas where we can expose our talents and thrive. Before I decided to follow my writing passion, my inner critic arose. It reminded me of all the reasons I would not succeed. Having the clarity and making the decision to write the book was all the success I needed. Everything else came after, but first I had to take the leap of faith. My desire to write was so strong I began writing without knowing what I would produce. I just let my heart carry my pen.

The world needs our talents, and our dreams will always materialize if we believe they will. Wishful thinking without inspired action will not be enough. However, when we follow our inner light, inspiration will guide us. Through guided inspiration, the answers to "what next?" *will* come. We will not tire so easily, and many things will unfold. For instance, you may grow within your job, having cultivated gratitude for your current position, and wind up transferring to a different position or being promoted. Being grateful for where you are now is a magnet for success. All it takes is becoming present enough to recognize opportunities, even if they appear in an unfamiliar guise.

The Path of Least Resistance

If you stay faithful to the exercises in this book, a breakthrough *will* occur. The problem comes when we wait for direct answers, and life does not work this way. Life is a beautiful collage and an intricate journey with many events and combinations at play. The potential within you is endless. If you allow yourself to listen, you will always be guided toward the path of least resistance. This is the path most aligned with the fulfillment of your desires, and it will flow smoothly. Your inner self knows well in advance what your desires are. You must make it easier by allowing life to unfold instead of forcing it to unfold the exact way your mind envisions it will.

In our society, we have been taught that forcing things and exerting our will over circumstances will bring us rewards. This statement is partially true. Yes, we must persist and exercise our will. However, it is easier to do the work when it is based on inspired enthusiasm. The reason we sometimes breeze through activities we find grueling at other times is because we are inspired in such a way that the process becomes easy. The impulses of desire and inspiration carry us easily through the task. Since you have not been trained to do so from an early age, there will be times when you cannot summon inspiration if a negative vibe pulls you away from the present moment. With a regular practice of present-moment awareness, you will learn how to set yourself up for success in the morning and begin the day renewed. Then, you will begin to notice imbalanced thoughts before they gain momentum and will be able to self-regulate by bringing yourself back to the now.

For the time being, you will be required to make forward movement no matter how you feel. Quitting is not the idea, but neither is forcing the answer. If you are present, intuitive answers will come to the rescue every time. The idea is to align yourself so you have more control over your feelings, which serve as your guidance system. Now that you have established a connection with your higher power and have "cleaned house," all you need to tap into your guidance system is to stay in present-moment awareness.

The maintenance and expansion of your spiritual life is critical to your success. Your soul will attract both what it loves and what it hates through the power of your attention. These two facets serve your soul's evolution. You will always make it harder for yourself if you attract negativity. You must be vigilant not to revert to lower vibrations and instead replace them with higher vibrations.

Remember, our thoughts control our destiny, and every thought that takes root will produce its kind. The shape of the world is formed through our thoughts. We can plant good seeds or bad seeds, but we guarantee their fruit. If we are unaware or creating by default, we will be baffled by the results and then might fall prey to victim mentality. Placing your life in the hands of your higher power will grant power many times stronger than you could have ever mustered on your own. You must align with this power and use it to the benefit of humankind. Each time you are guided and are able to take control of your thoughts and feelings, you are empowered with the master key system. It will become natural to you in time. You will become a transformative agent of destiny. If you continue to plant good seeds, the negative circumstances in your life will drop their arms and surrender.

Serving Others

Our highest purpose is to discover our true nature and help others discover theirs. *Finally, being grateful for the depth of your newfound awareness by following these spiritual principles, continue to help others and practice these principles throughout your life.*

No matter what activity you are inspired to do, your highest purpose is to serve others. This does not mean that you must become a teacher or a guru, although you can if you are so inspired. It means you must make it your life purpose to discover your true nature. In doing so, you will influence the world. Rare is the person who takes up the task of a fearless search to discover themselves. We are too preoccupied by the illusions of life. Our true space is within ourselves, and therein lies our true freedom and joy. You, my dear friend, are one of the brave ones and you will be handsomely compensated.

These beautiful steps are a wonderful beginning to experiencing true freedom. They will absolve you from your imagined confines of guilt and shame. It is time to move beyond what you've been to who you are. Once you are on your way, others will follow and the world will change. Be the change you wish to see in the world.

EXERCISE 10: CARRY THE MESSAGE TO OTHERS

The spiritual principle behind this final exercise is service. This exercise is a living one, and it has no end. It is as simple and as profound as this: *Never stop searching for the magnificent being you are.* Of course, we are meant to live and experience life, which involves love and pain, but none of these are our permanent states. The power that creates worlds lives within you. Money and fame will not get you there—only freedom from the bondage of self will. Yes, money and power can be wonderful allies because they can enable you to reach others, but they are not the way.

Once you have had a spiritual awakening as a result of the exercises in this book, carry the message to others. Practice these principles in all your affairs and help others set themselves free. It is everyone's noblest purpose to free others from the confines of their egos. You can lead the way by living your truth. When you dare to live an authentic life, you give others permission to do the same.

Share this book with a friend and help them through the exercises. If you've done them and they have worked for you, you can now support others through each of the steps. It is always beneficial to have a guide through the experience. Who we are is something we must each discover for ourselves, but we must also help each other on the journey.

CONCLUSION

I found out how the power of the universe and God lives within me, and that it is my desire to come into closer contact with this higher power each day. It is my heart's desire to share my experiences with others to help them find joy in this wonderful world. This life can be a veil of tears or a blissful experience. Be the change you wish to see in the world and help others overcome their pain. There will always be challenges, but you must learn how they are here to teach you lessons needed for your growth. Understand that pain is unavoidable, but suffering is optional. As humans, we did not sign up for an easy ride; we understood there would be challenges. When living by these spiritual principles, you will begin to see them as opportunities.

We must all learn to balance our mind's energy with our heart's energy. We are all learning and evolving, and we are in this together. It is my highest purpose to pass this message to you and to continue to help others find the freedom and satisfaction that is our birthright. Your satisfaction, freedom, and success will be in direct proportion to the measure of your honesty, the intent of your willingness, and your level of open-mindedness.

Life is a beautiful journey. You've practiced powerful spiritual principles that will help you throughout your life. You have done what few humans dare to—confront your ego with higher spiritual truths. Well done, brave one! This is the beginning of the end of suffering in a life-long journey toward growth and truth. You are on your way to discovering your true calling in life. Don't give up until the miracle happens.

Even if you don't have a clear answer, take heart in knowing the answers will come because you've put in the work. Many times, our answers come in divine timing, not our own desired timeframe. There are hundreds of combinations lining up for you, and you will have to decide when the moment comes to make the move that will mark your destiny. You have already begun by picking up this book and doing the work. Use these principles in all your affairs. You have constructed a blueprint by which to navigate through life. You don't have to wait to reach the summit to help others. Always help others along the way. Share your newfound knowledge. The fact you've done the work qualifies you to walk someone else through it. By helping others, your way will be made clear. You will become a light worker in this world. You are what we need most. Life has been waiting for you to become an active player in its unfolding. Thank you for showing up and rising to the occasion.

I am with you in heart and spirit, throughout your journey. We will surely meet again. Finally, never forget you are an eternal being who is beautiful and free.

Wishing you love, freedom, and the joy of living,

Sandra

ABOUT THE AUTHOR

Sandra P. Blanes is a successful entrepreneur and a spiritual life coach. Through her fifteen years' experience on her own spiritual journey, she has learned a system of seven steps to help seekers overcome their trepidations and discover a more meaningful and abundant life. Through the application of the spiritual principles contained in this book, she was able to overcome addictions, insecurities, depression, and cancer. Her mission in life is to help others apply foundational spiritual principles to their lives, regardless of their challenges. Her passions included meditation, traveling, and belly dancing, as well as spending time with her two children Natasha and Nicholas.

Visit her at www.sandrapblanes.com or sandra@sandrapblanes.com

Made in the USA
Las Vegas, NV
02 August 2024

93279817R00080

Introducing the Author

Paul W. Milhouse was born in St. Francisville, Illinois and received his first license to preach while a senior in Lawrenceville high school. He is a member of the Illinois Conference of The Evangelical United Brethren Church. Before coming to Harrisburg, Pennsylvania in 1951 as associate editor of the *Telescope-Messenger*, he served Evangelical United Brethren pastorates in Illinois. He has held many responsible positions in the communities where he has served as pastor and in his conference and denomination. This book, like his others, is characterized by its simple, direct and practical down-to-earth treatment of its subject.

CHRISTIAN WORSHIP

in

Symbol and Ritual

By

PAUL W. MILHOUSE

The Evangelical Press
Harrisburg, Pa.

Other Books by the Author

Enlisting and Developing Church Leaders
Come Unto Me
Except the Lord Build the House
Doorways to Spiritual Living

COPYRIGHT 1953
BY
PAUL W. MILHOUSE

Printed in the United States of America

DEDICATED TO

My fellow ministers in Illinois with whom I shared pastoral and conference responsibilities for many years,

in appreciation of

their friendship which has blessed my life and those worship experiences shared around camp fires, at Vesper Point and in sanctuaries through which I found inspiration and spiritual renewal.

FOREWORD

THERE is evidence of a new interest in worship among nonliturgical Protestant churches. It is recognized as a vital factor in the faith and life of Christian people. In recent years many church buildings have been remodeled for the purpose of making the sanctuary more suggestive of worship. There is a new interest in Christian symbols and rituals, and an increase in their use.

This new concern for worship is good. It could become an empty form or passing fad, however, unless both clergy and laity understand the historical background and development of worship. We must know its true meaning. We must know how to make proper use of the accepted symbols and rituals as aids in worship.

The first part of this book discusses the development of Christian worship and its essential elements. Part two is a study of the development of church buildings, Christian symbols, the Christian church calendar, the relationship of rituals to worship and those things appropriate in public worship. The purpose of these two sections is to give help toward a proper understanding and appreciation of public worship and the aids used in the service of worship. The third part of the book sets forth a brief interpretation of the major rituals of the Church and gives guidance in their proper use, so that they will be performed in a manner fitting to their purpose.

This book has been written for both laymen and ministers, to be used for personal reading and in study classes. It does not pretend to cover the subject in great detail but brings to the reader those things most needful for a general understanding and appreciation of Christian worship and the use of traditional aids in the act of public worship.

I am grateful to those who have taken time to read the manuscript and offer helpful suggestions: Bishop C. H. Stauffacher, Bishop G. E. Epp, Dr. Fay M. Bowman, Dr. Paul M. Herrick, Dr. Paul H. Eller, Dr. Paul R. Koontz, and Dr. D. H. Gilliatt; and to Miss Helen Shields who typed the manuscript for publication. Dr. Ralph M. Holdeman illustrated the symbols. I feel greatly indebted to others who have written on the subjects covered in this book.

This is sent forth with a humble prayer that readers may find it helpful in the enrichment of their worship experiences and that pastors may find it helpful in their parish ministry.

PAUL W. MILHOUSE.

Bible quotations from the American Revised Version used by permission.

TABLE OF CONTENTS

	Page
FOREWORD	5
INTRODUCTION BY BISHOP C. H. STAUFFACHER	11

Part One: Christian Worship

1. THE DEVELOPMENT OF CHRISTIAN WORSHIP 15

   The Temple—The Synagogue—Comparing Temple and Synagogue—The meetings of early Christians—Development of Christian worship—Church buildings—The Protestant Church

2. WHAT IS CHRISTIAN WORSHIP? 29

   The meaning of worship—Christian worship centers in Christ—Worship in the New Testament—The essence of Christian worship—What happens when we worship?

Part Two: Aids for Worship

3. THE PLACE WHERE WE WORSHIP 39

   The first church buildings—The architecture and arrangement of furnishings—The open chancel sanctuary—The pulpit-centered sanctuary

4. SOME SYMBOLS USED IN WORSHIP 49

   We find symbolism everywhere—The use of symbols—The more common symbols used in our churches

TABLE OF CONTENTS

                                                  Page

5. THE CHRISTIAN CALENDAR 63

    Its development — Churches differ in their use of it—The Christian year

6. ORDER AND RITUAL IN WORSHIP 71

    Three terms defined—Worship begins in fixing the mind on God—The goal of worship—Some general observations

7. LEADING OTHERS IN WORSHIP 77

    The responsibility—Music—The Scripture—The prayers—The sermon—Plan for every detail—The minister must prepare himself—The worshiper must prepare himself

8. WHAT IS APPROPRIATE IN WORSHIP? 85

    The purpose of this chapter—Candles—When reciting the Apostles' Creed—The Doxology and Gloria Patri—Prayers—The benediction—The open chancel sanctuary — The minister's dress

Part Three: The Use of Rituals

9. BAPTISM 97

    Baptism before Christ—Christian baptism—Infant baptism—The different forms of baptism—The baptismal service—The baptismal ritual

Table of Contents

		Page
10.	The Lord's Supper	103

What it is and its place in worship—Its institution—A ritual is developed for it—The Protestant emphasis—The Lord's Supper is a sacrament—The service of Holy Communion—The ritual—The minister must be spiritually prepared

| 11. | The Reception of Church Members | 111 |

The Church—Reception into the membership of a local church—The ritual

| 12. | Holy Matrimony | 119 |

Marriage is God's plan for human life—The Family—The marriage ceremony—Plans for the wedding—Details of the wedding service

| 13. | The Burial of the Dead | 127 |

The funeral service—The minister in charge

| 14. | Ordination | 131 |

What it is—The office of the Christian ministry—The work of the ministry—The ordination service

| 15. | Dedications and Installations | 135 |

The dedication of Church buildings—Installation services

INTRODUCTION

THE General Conference of The Evangelical United Brethren Church in session in Dayton, Ohio instructed the Commission on Ritual to prepare a book on the use of rituals in worship. "Christian Worship in Symbol and Ritual" is the fulfilment of that instruction.

The Commission on Ritual recognized the important place of rituals in the service of worship and the need for their meaningful and reverent use if they are to serve their purpose. With the increasing emphasis on worship in non-liturgical churches, rituals become significant aids. Their doctrinal contents must express the theology of the Church. Their statements of Christian faith must be clearly understood by the worshiper. Their use must be dignified, reverent and worshipful.

The Commission asked Dr. Paul W. Milhouse of Harrisburg, Pennsylvania to write this book. Doctor Milhouse is the associate editor of the *Telescope-Messenger*. He is the author of *Enlisting and Developing Church Leaders, Except the Lord Build the House,* and *Doorways to Spiritual Living*. This book comes out of his study of worship and his experience in leading congregations in worship. His own experience as a pastor in the use of rituals and his wide observation of their use have prepared him to render this service to the Church.

This book has been reviewed by the Commission on Rituals and is recommended for use in the churches. The Board of Bishops has approved the doctrinal contents of the book. The Commission is sure that it can be used with profit in study groups, mid-week services, women's societies, brotherhoods, youth fellowships, pastor's classes and in personal study. It goes forth with the hope and prayer of the Commission that it will assist both clergy and laity in making the use of our rituals more meaningful and worshipful.

C. H. STAUFFACHER, *Chairman.*

PART ONE

CHRISTIAN WORSHIP

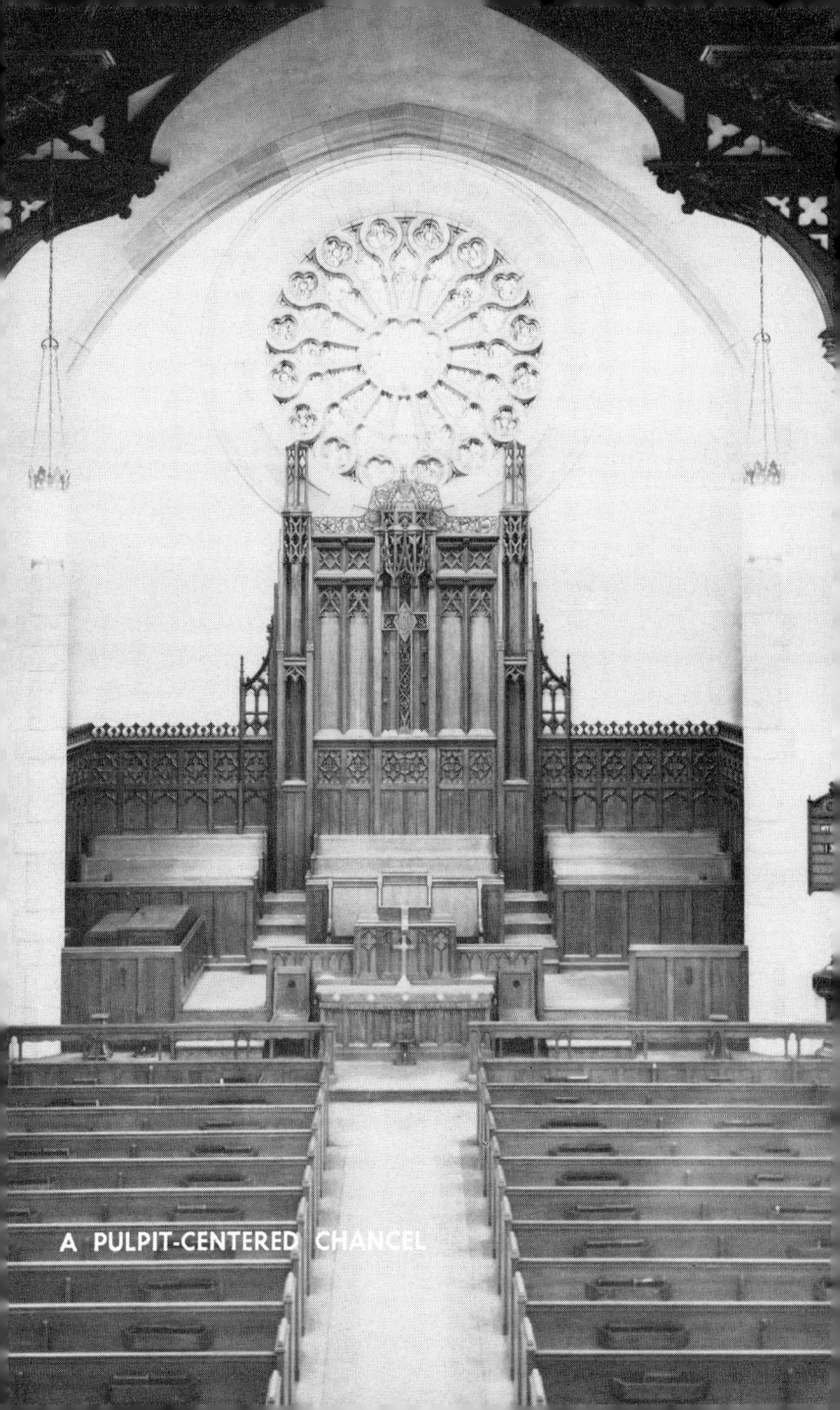

Chapter 1

THE DEVELOPMENT OF CHRISTIAN WORSHIP

THE first Christians were Jews, born and bred in the Jewish traditions of worship. It is not surprising therefore to find the roots of Christian worship running back to the Temple and to the synagogues.

The records indicate that Jesus went to the Temple on certain occasions to celebrate the religious festivals of his people. He also used the Temple as a place for teaching.[1] It was his custom to go to the synagogue on the Sabbath where he was sometimes invited to read the scriptures and interpret them.[2]

Many of the first generation Christians continued to visit the Temple and attend the synagogue services in their communities on certain occasions. When the apostles were on evangelistic tours they usually went first to the synagogue to preach.[3] Because of this close association in the beginning, one should not be surprised to find some features of worship as conducted in the Temple and synagogue services reflected in Christian worship.

The Temple was the national religious center for the Hebrew people. It was patterned after the movable Taber-

---

[1] Matthew 21: 23-42.
[2] Luke 4: 16-21.
[3] Acts 13: 5.

nacle which had been used as a place of worship during that period when the Israelites were wandering about from place to place in the arid lands of Sinai. This original Tabernacle was constructed of a wooden framework covered with skins. It was movable and similar to the tents in which the people lived. Every color and every appointment in this tent of worship had symbolic meaning. A curtain was set around it to separate it from the tents in which the people lived. A laver of brass in the open court provided for ceremonial washings which were suggestive of spiritual cleansing. A large altar provided for sacrifice. This altar stood before the door of the Tabernacle, and in this position called attention to sacrifice as an essential element of worship.

The Tabernacle itself was divided into two compartments. In the first and larger room were burning lamps and incense. Twelve loaves of bread were regularly kept on a table. All of these spoke of man in his worship of God.

The inside and smaller of the two compartments was called the Holy of Holies, in which was a wooden chest overlaid with gold, containing the stones upon which the Ten Commandments were written, a pot of manna and the rod which had been used by Aaron when assisting Moses in the leadership of the nation. The lid of the chest was plated with gold. Upon it were the figures of two cherubim.

This was in contrast to the religious customs of pagan people, for they put idols in their most holy places of worship. The Hebrews put into their holy place only those articles especially associated with their miraculous deliverance from Egypt and the establishment of their nation. These articles were not objects of worship but reminded the people of their dependance upon the mercy and redeeming power of God, and their covenant relationship with him.

At the heart of Hebrew worship was the idea of communion and fellowship with God, made possible through sacrifice. The individual provided the sacrifice and on his behalf, the priest offered it to God at the altar. The sinner's guilt was transferred to the animal through proper ritual. The worshiper thus depended upon the death of another to establish conditions for right relationships between himself and God.

When the Hebrew people settled in Palestine, more permanent types of homes were built to replace their tents. Established cities replaced their temporary encampments. A Temple was erected as a place of worship to replace the Tabernacle. Although in time the people scattered far from their holy city, many of the faithful ones made regular pilgrimages back to the Temple on the great festival days.

The synagogues came into existence during the time when the Temple at Jerusalem lay in ruins and many of the Israelites were living in forced exile from their native land. They had been taken to foreign lands by their conquerors. Victorious nations in ancient times often did this as a means of eliminating the possibility of revolt among people it had conquered.

When the Israelites no longer had a national center of worship and many were in exile, the faithful began meeting in their homes. Here they read from their sacred Scripture, sang some of the familiar psalms and prayed together for the strengthening of their common faith. The outgrowth of these meetings was the synagogue, a new institution among the Jewish people. The word means "to bring together in an assembly."

The synagogue building did not follow the pattern of the Temple. As far as the Israelites were concerned there was only one Temple. They longed to see it restored but they would not make copies of it or try to build another in some other city. The synagogue was designed as a place of assembly where the people of the community could hear the reading of the Law and the Prophets. Each synagogue became the religious center of its community. Here the rabbi instructed the children in the religious heritage of the nation.

A very informal order of service was developed for the synagogue in keeping with its purpose. It usually consisted of the singing of psalms, and the offering of prayers. The scriptures were read and interpreted by the local rabbi or some visiting teacher. He also exhorted the people to obey the Law.

A synagogue came to be established in every community where there were enough people to support one, but these synagogues never took the place of the Temple which was in Jerusalem. It was a new institution created to meet the religious needs of a people who were exiled from home and without a central place of worship. In later years when the Temple was restored, the synagogue continued, but the faithful made long journeys in order to be in Jerusalem on certain festival occasions so that they might worship in the Temple.

Comparing the Temple and synagogues, we find that the Temple had an altar but no pulpit. The synagogue had a pulpit but no altar. The Temple service centered in sacrifice. The synagogue had no place for sacrifice. Its service centered in instruction. The Temple had no provision for instruction except as it might take place in the courts. The teaching of religion was mainly the responsibility of the parents.[4]

With no altar in the synagogue and no provision for sacrifice, a new emphasis came into worship. Throughout Israel's

---

[4] Deuteronomy 11: 18-21.

history the prophets had insisted that the sacrifice of animals was not sufficient and warned that religion could decay even while the priests were regularly offering sacrifices. The synagogue provided opportunity for instruction and a renewed emphasis upon the spiritual element so essential in all true worship.

The leader of the synagogue service was usually a layman who had been elected president of the congregation. The rabbi who gave the interpretation of the Scripture was not a priest but a scholar. He offered no sacrifice but instructed the people in the Word of God. Since an understanding of God and obedience to his will are essentials to right relationships with him, preaching and exhortation were recognized as important elements in worship.

There was order in synagogue worship but no fixed ritual as in the case of worship in the Temple. The building was very plain with religious symbols at a minimum. The reading desk was central because the Scripture and its interpretation was central in the service. Behind the reading desk was the storage cabinet for the scrolls which was called the Ark of the Covenant. This was probably suggested by the arrangement of the Temple which had the Ark of the Covenant in the Holy of Holies.

Worship implies an awareness of God's presence, but God becomes real to people only through a personal experience of him. An awareness of the divine Presence is a matter of the mind and heart, not of the physical senses. Preaching was given a prominent place in the synagogue because through it, the individual could be informed and guided in his thinking so as to be aware of God.

Temple worship was rich in symbolism that emphasized important truths associated with man's salvation, but the synagogue furnished a channel for a spiritual emphasis which the Temple did not have, thus providing a pattern which could easily be converted to Christian worship.

The meetings of the early Christians were not planned to conform to some standard established by the Church but were the natural outgrowth of the common fellowship and experience of these early disciples. Although some of the Jewish Christians of the first century continued to go to the Temple and synagogue on various occasions, it became a common practice for Christians to meet in their local communities on Sundays, probably in the evenings. The first day of the week was chosen because it was on this day that Jesus arose from the grave. Among the Christians, Sunday was often referred to as the *Lord's Day*.

These Sunday meetings of the Christians were held in their homes. Here they shared experiences and a period of fellowship that often included an observance of the Lord's Supper. Such meetings strengthened their faith and provided a means for expressing and cultivating their oneness in Christ and with each other.

For the Christians, Sunday soon came to be more important than the Jewish Sabbath. They considered it to be the more logical day for Christian worship. It became a general practice to assemble on Sunday for the purpose of worshiping God in the light of what Jesus had taught. These meetings followed the pattern of the synagogue. There was praise and prayer. Selections from the Old Testament were read and discussed in the light of their experience of Christ. There was singing of psalms.

The Christian services of worship were not the same as the synagogue services, even though they followed the general pattern of the synagogue. Distinctive Christian features were added. In addition to the Law and the Prophets, the letters of Paul and of the other apostles were read if copies were available. Whenever they were fortunate enough to have one of the manuscripts which gave an account of Christ's life and ministry, selections were read from it. Older persons in the group would often share some personal experience they had had with the Christ. In addition to the psalms, Christian hymns were used. It soon became common practice to celebrate the Lord's Supper regularly. The meetings closed with the benediction and the kiss of peace.

Early Christian worship centered in spiritual fellowship with Jesus Christ. The first disciples missed his presence more than any other single thing. Meeting together to talk about him and his teachings made him seem near again. But these assemblies were not merely memory sessions. Fellowship with Christ was a reality. They experienced the fulfillment of his words, "When two or three are gathered together in my name, there am I in the midst of them." [5] This personal experience of fellowship with Christ is the essence of Christian worship.

It is easy, therefore, to see why the synagogue service rather than the Temple service furnished the pattern for Christian worship. Christians at worship are not spectators but participants. They are disciples of Jesus Christ meeting together in a mutual sharing and corporate expression of their faith in God and personal experience of his power and presence through Christ. Christian worship thus not only exalts God through appropriate praise and adoration but becomes a strengthening force in the Christian's life. Such worship rests in and grows out of personal fellowship with Christ. This fellowship is most completely expressed and symbolized in the Lord's Supper.

---

[5] Matthew 18: 20.

Christian worship developed with the Lord's Supper becoming its most complete symbol. It took a central place because it expresses the principle fact upon which spiritual fellowship with God depends. It is a memorial of Christ's death in which something took place that was essential for the redemption of man and the removal of the barrier of sin, making fellowship possible between man and God.

One might readily assume that these early Christians would have celebrated the Lord's Supper on the anniversary of its institution, which would have been on Thursday according to the most generally accepted calculations. But they did not select that day. Neither did they keep it on the anniversary of Christ's death, which would have been Friday. They chose to celebrate it on the first day of the week, the day when Christ arose from the grave. They selected this day because it was the resurrection that gave meaning to his death. If there had been no resurrection, Christ's death would apparently have been the same as that of any other good man. His death cannot be understood apart from his resurrection. In this way two very important points of Christian faith were united. The use of Sunday as a day of worship and the celebration of the Lord's Supper became two distinctive marks of Christian worship.

As congregations grew and public services became more common, the sermon increased in importance. It no longer remained an informal talk to help Christians live their faith, but became an organized discourse for the purpose of giving information about the Christian faith to those who were not believers, with the express purpose of converting them to Christianity. It became an important evangelistic channel and the speaker preached for a decision. He confronted his hearers with Christ and exhorted them to become his disciples. The sermon is still one of the most important instruments of evangelism.

According to most historians, the non-Christians were dismissed after the sermon and the Christians remained to celebrate the Lord's Supper. It may have become a general practice in some places to hold two services on Sunday after Christianity became more generally accepted throughout the Roman Empire. Where this was true, the morning service continued with emphasis upon instruction and the evening service was primarily an assembly of Christians for the celebration of the Lord's Supper. These meetings were often held in their homes. For the evening meeting they would eat together, then the Lord's supper was celebrated.

Whether the celebration of the Lord's Supper took place in a home or in a public service of worship, the worshipers supplied the elements. The bread and wine brought by the people were properly consecrated and used in the sacrament. This was their contribution or offering to the service.

In time it became the practice of the worshipers to bring money for the offering, instead of or in addition to food and clothing. This offering represented the worshiper's response to God's gift of Jesus Christ as Savior. It was a giving of one's substance for the nourishment of others as Christ gave himself for the spiritual nourishment of man. Christ's gift of himself is ceremonially expressed in the celebration of the Lord's Supper. Man's gift of himself is partially expressed in the giving of his possessions as an offering to God which is used under the direction of the Church for Christian purposes.

As the Church moved into other countries and as people of these lands came into leadership, different ways of thinking naturally reflected itself in the services of worship. During the third century liturgical forms appeared and the service was divided into two parts, the "Liturgy of the Catechumens" and the "Liturgy of the Faithful." The first included praise, prayer, singing and the sermon. It was designed for instruction in the Christian faith. Non-Christians were then dismissed. The second part was especially for the Christians and centered in the celebration of the Lord's Supper. Since fellowship with the living Christ is the highest experience of Christian worship, the sacrament of the Lord's Supper was central in the service and was usually placed at the close as a climax of the worship experience.

Church buildings came to be erected for Christian worship as the number of Christians in local communities increased. The first services of Christian worship were held in the homes of the people, but as their numbers increased their homes became too small. They had to seek larger assembly halls. When persecution became less severe, church buildings were erected.

The first church buildings were probably constructed along the style of the people's homes, for Christian worship had begun in the home. The order of service was very informal and spontaneous, easily fitting into a home-like atmosphere. The first Christian literature was letters which the Apostles wrote to the Christian congregations of different communities. These were read and then circulated among other congregations.

Later development of church buildings followed the pattern of the Roman basilica. This was a rectangular building used as a court or assembly. It had developed originally after the pattern of royal palaces in common use at that time. Entrance was at one end and a raised platform was at the other. This platform was usually recessed in the form of a half circle. Here sat the judges and others who might be sharing in the leadership of the assembly. The king and his personal advisors occupied this space in the royal palace. The main floor of the building was for the people. Between the place where the people assembled and the elevation where the presiding officers were, was a space called the transept. The word means "to hedge in," and was used in the sense of separating the platform area from the main floor. An arrangement such as this could easily be converted to Christian worship and soon came to be used as the pattern for most church buildings. The transept was often extended to give the building the form of a cross.

The Protestant Church emerged as a revolt against the corrupt practices of the Church in Europe during the Middle Ages. The Church had become associated with political corruption. Preaching was neglected. Worshipers were often little more than spectators to a performance conducted by the priest. A system of penance had been developed which led to the selling of indulgences.

During the fourteenth and fifteenth centuries, strong protests against religious corruption and spiritual emptiness began to be voiced. By the early part of the sixteenth century these protests had become so strong that they could no longer be ignored by those in authority. Instead of reforming, however, they denounced those who protested, excommunicated them and persecuted them.

This forced the reformers, and those who supported their views, to organize new congregations. The purpose was to establish local fellowships of Christians along patterns that would restore the purity of faith and consecrated devotion of the first century disciples. It was not an effort to establish a new religion but an endeavor to witness to Christianity in its purest and truest form. These people came to be known as Protestants and this was the beginning of the Protestant Church. The word means to "witness forth" (*pro*-forth, *testari*-to witness), a solemn affirmation of faith. In common usage it has come to designate that portion of the Church which refuses to submit to the Roman Catholic Church.

Although we speak of the Protestant Church as the result of the Reformation, the source of its stream of life is found in the Church of the first century. It is not a division of the Catholic Church in the strict sense of the word. It is the result of a new outburst of spiritual faith and life which could not satisfactorily express itself through the forms of worship and the faith patterns developed by the Roman Church of the fifteenth and sixteenth centuries. Its real beginning is in the first century with Christ and the gospel he preached.

Distinctive characteristics of the Protestant Church are its emphasis upon the inner life and the central place the sermon occupies in worship. Christianity is first of all a thing of mind and heart. It begins with a decision of the mind that dedicates the heart. It is not a new set of rules for living but a new life. One does not become a Christian by learning a creed but through a surrender of life to Christ. This brings about a spiritual transformation that is nothing short of a new birth. To be a Christian is to be in that faith relationship with God which puts Christ at the center and in control of the human heart, mind and will.

The Protestant Church has always made preaching an essential part of worship because preaching informs the mind, warms the heart and influences the will. Religion must touch all of life. If religion is only a mental attitude it may be a philosophy but it is not likely to be a passion or conviction that disciplines conduct. A religion that touches only the heart is emotionalism and will lack wisdom to guide its expression. If there is no dedication of will to God, religion has neither spirit nor power to give life meaning or reason for existence. Preaching is important in guiding individuals and groups in meaningful worship and holy living. Protestantism restored the sermon to a place of importance in worship.

Chapter 2

WHAT IS CHRISTIAN WORSHIP?

ALTHOUGH the Bible gives no formal definition of worship, it makes more than twelve hundred references to the act of worship. The two Hebrew words most frequently used in the Old Testament with reference to worship express the idea of a reverent attitude in both mind and body. They indicate a prostration of oneself before a superior in an act of reverent adoration. The Greek words used in the New Testament also indicate reverent devotion and include the idea of service to God. Our English word worship comes from the Anglo-Saxon and combines the idea of worth with the suffix indicating a state or relationship. Worship is a recognition of the *worth-ship* of God.

Worship indicates those acts and words through which man appropriately expresses reverent devotion toward God as the supreme Being worthy of all honor and adoration. The act is motivated by the belief that God, although unseen and far superior to man, is nevertheless actively interested in man and his relationships. It is based upon the conviction that communion can take place between the creature and the Creator, and that this communion is important to the fulfillment of the creature's life.

The pattern of worship depends to a large measure upon the faith of the individual and of the group to which he belongs. Worship is man's response to an awareness of God in a manner that honors God as being of first importance and highest in authority.

Christian worship centers in Christ, for he is central in the Christian faith. The Christian thinks of God in terms of Christ. He is the way to God, the door which gives access to the Father.[1] He is God incarnate and so through him God is revealed to us in terms of human relationships. The will of God is made known through Christ who is our Savior. Surrender of heart and will to Christ brings redemption from sin and puts life under the directing influence of the Holy Spirit. Christian faith and Christian living center in Christ; so must Christian worship.

Jesus did not give his disciples formal instructions regarding worship, but there is evidence that he considered it very important. It was his custom to go to the synagogue regularly and we find him making visits to the Temple on holy days. On one occasion he said, "But the hour cometh, and now is, when the true worshipers shall worship the Father in spirit and truth: for such doth the Father seek to be his worshipers. God is a spirit, and they that worship him must worship in spirit and truth." [2]

Jesus was talking with a Samaritan woman at the time he spoke those words. They were given in answer to a question which she asked concerning the proper place to worship, for the Samaritans, like the Hebrews, had been much concerned about the place dedicated to worship. In the Old Testament the procedures considered proper in worship were carefully described in full detail, even to the clothing of the priests. The animal to be used for sacrifice had to meet certain specifications. The act of sacrifice had to be according to the rules of the ritual.

---

[1] John 10: 10.

[2] John 4: 23, 24.

The yearly cycle of festivals was very important in Old Testament worship. The Temple was the center of worship for the nation. The faithful made regular pilgrimages to worship there on stated occasions. The place and the ritual were considered of major importance.

The sacrifice presented in worship was payment to God of what was due him as Creator and an acknowledgement of his Lordship. It was also a confession of sin in which man admitted his need of God's forgiveness to establish and maintain proper relationships between himself and the Creator. The end of Old Testament worship was fellowship and it was believed that the only basis upon which this could be established between a holy God and a sinful man was sacrifice—the giving of a life that was innocent on behalf of one which was guilty. It was an acknowledgement that a sinner can not save himself but is dependent upon what another does on his behalf.

A study of worship in the New Testament reveals the emphasis to be upon the spiritual elements rather than upon the physical. Jesus always stressed the spiritual. His classic statement on worship is probably that one made to the Samaritan woman, "God is spirit and they that worship him must worship in spirit and truth." [3] He condemned religious leaders who emphasized the externals of worship more than the spiritual.

The records indicate that early Christian worship was characterized by spontaneity and freedom of expression. There appears to be no special order or ritual for the services. Believers came together for mutual fellowship, conscious of Christ's spiritual presence among them according to his prom-

---

[3] John 4: 24.

ise, "Where two or three are gathered together in my name, there am I in the midst of them." [4]

The essence of Christian worship is personal communion with God. There is no record that animal sacrifice was ever associated with Christian worship, even though its roots go back into the Old Testament in which animal sacrifice is prominent.

The New Testament talks about spiritual sacrifice. "I beseech you therefore, brethren, by the mercies of God, to present your bodies a living sacrifice, holy, acceptable to God, which is your spiritual service." [5] The human body is not to be burned but is to be dedicated in obedient service to God. One is to dedicate himself to God as completely as if laid on the altar as a sacrifice. As in Old Testament worship, so in Christian worship, the climax comes at the moment when life is given to God. Christian worship is not complete until human life is dedicated to obedient service and impelled by consecrated devotion.

Christian worship is therefore not something that can be done for the worshiper by a priest ministering at an altar, but something the worshiper does under the guidance and with the assistance of the minister. According to the Scripture, every individual believer has the right of direct access to God. We need no earthly priest as a mediator between us and God. Christ is our eternal intercessor in heaven. Ministers are ordained to minister in Christ's name for the purpose of giving guidance and assistance to worshipers in presenting themselves as living sacrifices to God through faith in Jesus Christ. Only such dedication of life as this puts one in right relationship with God.

---

[4] Matthew 18: 20.
[5] Romans 12: 1.

This means that rituals and all physical elements associated with worship are less important than the spiritual relationship of the worshiper with God. Buildings, symbols, and rituals can aid or hinder worship. They are important but are not the most important things. True worship can take place under many different conditions and apart from any special building, altar or symbol, but it must have guidance if it is to be meaningful and direct the worshiper in a true experience of fellowship with God. Christian worship is a recognition of God's supreme worth in words and acts that are in harmony with the revelation which God has given through Jesus Christ.

What Happens When We Worship? Worship fixes the mind upon God. At the very beginning of the act, words of Scripture, prayers and hymns turn one's thoughts to God. The worship service in the church provides time for prayerful thinking about our Heavenly Father under the guidance of a minister of the gospel. It makes us aware of divine power, love and holiness, and guides us in responding with reverent devotion to him who is Lord over all.

Worship provides us with a spiritual observation point. In the act of worship life is brought before God and critically viewed in the light of revealed truth. The thoughts of the mind, the passions of the heart, and the deeds of the body as expressed in daily conduct are evaluated according to God's will. Conscience is quickened with an awareness of sin and failure when one stands in the presence of perfect Holiness and Love. In worship we come to a spiritual observation point which enables us to see life as God sees it.

Worship frees us from moral powerlessness. When we see ourselves in the light of God's judgment, we recognize our sin as rebellion against our Creator. Cleansing from sin comes only through the forgiveness of God made possible by our confession and repentance of sin. Assurance of forgiveness comes through the acceptance of God's Word. This assurance brings inner peace to the worshiper, restores spiritual fellowship with God, and frees one from moral impotency. Ideals are reaffirmed. The burden of guilt is lifted. Right purposes are strengthened.

Worship heals the illness of the soul. Inner conflicts cease when life is completely surrendered in obedience to the will of God. Principles and practices are correlated. Rebellious desires are brought under control. Conduct is directed in paths of righteousness. Wrong attitudes are replaced by right ones. Motives are purified by the cleansing power of the Holy Spirit.

Worship strengthens our faith in God because it brings us into a personal experience of fellowship with him. We are not limited to what others tell us about God but personally experience his Presence and Power. Worship makes God more real and personal. We walk out of the sanctuary with new confidence and assurance that God is the answer to our needs.

Worship leads to better living. Conscious guilt and conflict weakens our ability for right living, but confession of sin brings forgiveness and lifts the weight of our guilt. Worship is not only an acknowledgement of God's supremacy but in the act of worship, we also admit that we are inadequate within ourselves to meet all of our needs. We turn to Another and bring life to him for help. We leave the service of worship with renewed purpose to follow where God leads and are empowered by the Holy Spirit through a dedication of life to God.

Worship makes one conscious of God's purpose for human life. This gives meaning to existence and determines the direction toward which life must move in fulfillment of God's will. One emerges from an experience of worship with the conviction that certain things are required if one is to know the joy and satisfaction of life's fulfillment according to God's purpose.

Worship brings new visions of eternal things. We see more clearly what God wants us to be and do. The things of life are evaluated in the light of that which is eternal, and to these things life is dedicated.

PART TWO

AIDS FOR WORSHIP

AN OPEN CHANCEL SANCTUARY

Chapter 3

THE PLACE WHERE WE WORSHIP

THE first Christians had no special buildings for worship. They met together in their homes. As the number of Christians in a community increased, more commodious quarters became necessary. In some instances, halls or larger rooms were added to privately owned houses.

The first church buildings were erected during the second century. These were very plain and were patterned after the people's homes. They were called churches, a Greek word meaning the "Lord's house." These were houses dedicated to the worship of God. They were places where the Christians of the community could meet for fellowship and worship. Their meetings were like a family of children gathering at the Father's house.

During periods of persecution Christians often had to meet secretly and at night, in caves and in underground burial places to evade their enemies. The practice of building churches did not become common until the fourth century after persecution had ceased.

When Constantine officially accepted the Christian faith, the Christians were granted freedom of worship and the protection of the Roman government. This removed the stigma from Christianity in the eyes of many and converts increased. In order to have places large enough for their assemblies, it became necessary for the Christians to rent public halls or erect buildings especially for worship. In some instances pagan temples were converted into churches. Some pagan temples were torn down and churches were erected in their place.

The church buildings which were erected from this time on followed the general pattern of the public buildings of the Romans. These were rectangular in shape. One end was usually in the form of a semicircle with an elevation. The leaders of the meeting or the judges of the court sat here while presiding over the assembly.

When the Christians followed this pattern for their churches, they put a table at the elevated end and placed a chair behind it. This was called the communion table and the chair was called the bishop's chair. This was the term used to designate the presiding officer at the communion service. On either side of the bishop's chair were other seats for the presbyters. These were the men who had general supervision over the affairs of the Christian group in the community. The interior of these first churches was very plain.

The artistic elements in church buildings came as a later development. They served two purposes. They were means of conveying religious truth to the worshipers and they made the plain buildings more attractive. The Bible was not generally available to people for private reading in those days. There were very few copies in existence and these were expensive because they were hand written on parchment. Pictures and symbols were developed as means of instructing people in religious truth. Pictures in church windows, sculptured figures and paintings became highly developed arts. Symbols of the Christian faith were interwoven into curtains and used on the furnishings.

THE PLACE WHERE WE WORSHIP 41

The architecture and arrangement of the furnishings of the church building were made to represent Christian truths. Since the semicircular end of the church was used by the clergy, it came to be known as the *chancel*. The word itself means a screened enclosure and its use probably came from the practice of marking off this section with a lattice-like fence or rail, separating it from the main part of the floor. As choirs came to be used in the service of worship, they were often given a place in the chancel with the clergy since their task was to share in the leadership of worship.

The main body of the public hall after which the church building was patterned, was called the *nave*. This is where the worshipers assembled and so the word is used to indicate the main floor occupied by the people. Between the chancel and the place where the worshipers assembled was an open space. This space was often extended in both directions at right angles to the main hall, giving to the floor of the building the effect of a cross. This was called the *transept*. The word means literally "across hedge," and was used in this instance because it extended across the front of the chancel. The *spire* came to be a distinctive characteristic of the church, symbolizing the message of the gospel as pointing men's thoughts upward to God.

There has never been complete uniformity in church buildings and there are many different patterns in use today. Some are very simple and plain while others are elaborately decorated with religious symbols and pictures. The outside architecture varies from the stately spire and cathedral style buildings to structures that appear very similar to other buildings in the community. The interior furnishings also vary. Some are straight and others are square with curved pews.

Some have center aisles and others do not. In spite of the many differences in church buildings, they can generally be classified according to their arrangement in relationship to the chancel from which the service of worship is conducted.

The church building that has a communion table or altar at the back of the chancel with a pulpit on one side and a lectern on the other is called an *open chancel church*. The term "open-chancel" is used because the chancel rail is open at the center and the central aisle runs into the chancel, giving the effect of an open and unhindered approach to the altar or communion table at the back. The church that has a speaker's desk or pulpit in the center of the elevated section is called a *pulpit-centered church*. Both arrangements are rich in history and tradition. Both symbolize important religious truths associated with Christian worship.

The open chancel sanctuary with the communion table at the center symbolizes the central place which spiritual communion and fellowship with God has in the experience of worship. This was the arrangement in the earliest church buildings. The pulpit was added to the chancel because preaching was recognized as a very important factor in Christian worship. A lectern was later placed on the other side of the chancel opposite the pulpit to provide a place for the Bible. The public reading of the Bible takes place here. The service is also conducted from the lectern.

The central aisle leading directly to the communion table reminds the worshipers of their free and direct access to God without need of any priest as mediator. The communion table is usually approached by a series of three steps. These are interpreted to represent the Holy Trinity, the Father, the Son, and the Holy Spirit. Some interpret them to represent faith, hope and love.

This arrangement of the chancel symbolizes the relationship of the sermon to the act of worship. The minister's message is to assist the worshiper in his personal experience of communion with God. The sermon presents God, interprets his will to the people and gives instruction that will enable the individual to personally commune with his Creator.

The open chancel sanctuary with the altar at the center reflects the Old Testament emphasis upon sacrifice. The altar of burnt offerings occupied a conspicuous place in the court of the ancient Tabernacle. It stood before the entrance to the holy place. Sacrifice was the chief characteristic of worship in the Tabernacle and in the Temple that succeeded it. There was no pulpit nor provision for preaching. Religious instruction was mainly the responsibility of the home.

The idea of sacrifice is basic in the establishment of right relationships between God and sinful man. Sin is destructive to man and separates him from God. It prevents him from being what God intended him to be and creates a barrier that cuts him off from spiritual fellowship with his Creator. Man cannot remove this sin from his own life because it is a part of himself. It is not simply a wrong act, but includes the attitude and desire of the heart which initiated the wrong act, and these attitudes and desires are inseparable from the individual himself. If the barrier caused by sin is to be removed and spiritual fellowship is to be restored between God and man, God must do it. Man is not sufficient for it.

God can remove sin only as life is given to him. When the worshiper came to the Tabernacle he brought an animal for a sin offering. Through proper ceremony his sin was confessed and laid upon the animal. The animal thus became a sin-bearer and was sacrificed to God. The death of the animal was a substitute for the sinner and through it he gave himself to God. It was an acknowledgement that man can not atone for his sin but must depend upon a sacrifice made on his behalf.

The presence of an altar emphasizes the association of sacrifice with worship. The bloody sacrifices of Tabernacle and Temple worship would be a shocking sight to Christians. Animal sacrifice was never associated with Christian worship, but from the first, Christ has been thought of in terms of sacrifice. His death has always been looked upon as a death for sinners. It is associated with man's redemption. The Bible declares that "Christ died for us." This fact can never be separated from Christian worship. In this arrangement, both the idea of sacrifice and the importance of preaching are recognized. The altar-centered arrangement for the sanctuary developed early.

Churches began to be built without a central altar following the Reformation as a reaction against anything that was similar to the Roman Church which had become associated with spiritual corruption in the thinking of many. The idea of sacrifice then came to be expressed through sermon, prayer, song and sacrament, for sacrifice is essential in Christian faith and worship.

In the altar-centered church, the open center aisle and divided communion rail give the worshiper a clear view of the altar. This reminds him that he has direct access to God apart from any human mediator, but this meeting of God and man takes place at the point where life is given to God, and at that point there is always an altar.

Churches that have no central altar refer to the chancel rail as an altar, and there men come to give themselves to God and God meets them there in redeeming grace. It is a place of prayer, because prayer is associated with dedication of life. It also becomes a place for the celebration of the sacraments for these, too, are acts of sacrifice.

The divided choir arrangement gives the choir a position as part of the congregation at worship rather than performers who are the center of attraction.

Protestants accept the Bible as the supreme authority of the church. In the open chancel arrangement, it has a place on the lectern. In the pulpit-centered arrangement, it is on the speaking desk. It is the Word of God, the source book for the preacher's sermon. It is a record of men's experience and reaction to divine revelation. It is the source of Christian truth.

The pulpit-centered sanctuary emphasizes the important place of preaching in worship. Christian worship is essentially spiritual communion between God and the individual. If true worship is to take place, the individuals in the congregation need guidance and instruction to properly condition them for communion with God. Preaching is the channel through which this instruction and guidance can best be given. Through the sermon, the preacher proclaims God's message to man, interprets its meaning in relationship to faith and conduct, and gives counsel to assist worshipers in bringing themselves into those attitudes and relationships that will assure them of divine grace and blessing.

The sermon is a very important act of worship because through it, the word of God is personalized. It becomes a living voice with passion, love, faith, judgment and challenge. Through it the heart of the worshiper is prepared for and guided in a dedication of life to God.

The pulpit-centered church follows the tradition of the synagogue in which the first Christian messages were preached.

The synagogue was planned as a place for preaching. There the Law was read and interpreted. Instead of having an altar like that of the Temple for the offering of sacrifices, there was a speaker's platform elevated high enough for the speaker to be seen and heard by the people. The reading of the Law and its interpretation were the chief acts that took place during the service.

Preaching was very important in the early life of the Church. It was the chief instrument through which converts were won to the Christian faith. It was the medium through which people were made aware of spiritual needs and told of God's redeeming grace. The first Apostles went about the country preaching in the synagogues, on the street corners and in homes. Although many of the early informal gatherings of Christians were in homes, there was always a place for consideration of the meaning of the gospel for everyday living. As it became a more common practice to hold public services in church buildings, preaching was given an even more important place.

Whenever preaching has been neglected, the Church has become weak and usually corrupt in both faith and conduct. The Reformation restored preaching to a central place of importance in Christian worship, because the reformers knew that this was necessary to counteract spiritual corruption. Preaching is essential if worship is to be intelligent, spiritually pure, and related to life. With this renewed emphasis on preaching, many of the Protestant churches made the pulpit central in the chancel.

Preaching will always be important in Christian worship because it is a most effective means of informing the mind of truth essential for intelligent worship and a means of persuading the heart to give to God what is due him. The end of worship is personal communion with God. This is a spiritual experience, not a physical relationship, and is therefore more dependent upon the condition of the mind and heart than upon physical surroundings or ritualistic procedure. "God is a spirit: and they that worship him must worship in spirit and in truth." [1] Preaching is the means by which the minister of the gospel prepares the minds and hearts of the worshipers to give themselves as a living sacrifice to God, dedicated to him in worship and service.[2]

The place where men worship ought to be treated with great reverence. It is dedicated to God and it is here that men meet God. Of course God needs no house in which to dwell and spirit cannot be confined to four walls, but man needs a place set apart from others where his thoughts will be directed to God and in which he will find an atmosphere helpful to worship.

---

[1] John 4: 24.
[2] Romans 12: 1.

Chapter 4

SOME SYMBOLS USED IN WORSHIP

THE word symbol is derived from two Greek words that literally mean "throw together." A symbol is a design or picture that throws together an abstract idea and a visible sign that suggests the idea. Symbols are objects that represent something else, not by exact resemblance but by suggestion or association of thought.

We find symbolism everywhere. The words used in writing are symbols. They do not even resemble the objects they represent, but this is preferred to picture writing which is clumsy and limited in its use. A flag represents a nation and a salute to it represents devotion to that nation, not simply reverence for a piece of cloth. The handshake is a symbol of friendship. A uniform is symbolic of service in an organization or a profession which the uniform represents. A church building suggests Christian faith and worship. It would be a strange thing if religion had no symbolism.

The Bible is rich in symbolism and from a very early period in the life of the Church, Christians have made use of signs and symbols. Some of them may have originated as a secret code language in times of persecution and in situations where individuals would be in danger if it were known that they were Christians. Symbols were the first visual aids used for teaching Christian doctrines. Missionaries used symbols as a bridge over the barriers caused by differences in language. Some Christian symbols may have developed out of a desire to add some ornamental decoration to the plain sanctuary. The idea of incorporating Christian truth in these embellishments gave birth to ornamental designs and figures that were symbolic of the Christian faith. Such designs or figures can be helpful in conditioning the thoughts of the congregation for worship by fixing the mind on the spiritual things represented by the symbols.

The use of symbols, however, gives no assurance that the minds of those who see them will always think of what the symbols represent. Spiritual worship is conditioned by the state of mind and the attitude of the heart more than by the physical furnishings of the building. Protestantism has never made extensive use of symbols. Many Protestant church buildings are very plain and the use of symbols is considered by many to be excessive and useless baggage, unnecessary ornaments.

The Medieval Church fell into corruption through a neglect of preaching and an over-emphasis upon the observance of sacraments and the use of rituals in worship. Without instruction to guide the mind and heart, rituals and sacraments become meaningless and ineffective as aids to worship. They cease to be channels of spiritual blessing when it is assumed that they have some supernatural power in themselves.

The Protestant reformers insisted that preaching is essential to spiritual worship and that a knowledge of the Bible is necessary for Christian living. For this reason the Protestant Church has always given much attention to Bible instruction and has promoted education for all people. Preaching is more prominent than sacrament. Ritual is servant to the needs of the people.

Protestantism has sometimes had a tendency to be heavy on the intellectual side because of its emphasis upon right thinking as essential to right conduct and worship. We must remember that worship is not only an act of the mind, but includes the heart and will. The end of worship is not a holy act but a holy life. Living is determined and directed by the decisions of the will, but the will is motivated by both mind and heart. The mind requires only a written and spoken language for its work but the heart is often stirred by what is seen, felt or heard. Because of these facts, Protestantism has never completely discarded symbolism.

The more common symbols of the Christian faith should be known and understood by all Christians if they are to have meaning and be properly used as aids in worship. Unless symbols have meaning for those who use them, they are only useless ornaments.

The cross is the most used symbol. It recalls Christ's death at Calvary and his resurrection out of the tomb. Because Christ's death and resurrection are central facts in the Christian religion, the cross has become the major symbol of that faith. It is used to mark the graves of Christians, indicating the hope of eternal life through the resurrection of Christ. It is the insignia of Christian chaplains in the armed services. It is used to distinguish churches from other buildings.

The plain LATIN CROSS is the most familiar. It has been estimated by some that there are 400 different forms of the cross. The form which has three elevations at the base is called the GRADED CROSS. The three elevations represent faith, hope and love in descending order—"the greatest of these is love."[1] ST. ANDREW'S CROSS is in the form of the letter x. It is said that Andrew requested crucifixion on this kind of a cross because he did not feel worthy to die on the same kind

---

[1] I Corinthians 13: 13.

of a cross upon which Jesus died. The MALTESE CROSS is in the form of four spearheads meeting at a central point. The eight outer points symbolize the beautitudes. It was first used by the Knights of St. John on the island of Malta.

The cross with the letters I.N.R.I. on a banner across the top is a reminder of Pilate's inscription above the head of Christ. Each letter is the first letter in each of the Latin words, "Jesus of Nazareth, King of the Jews." The letters IHS on the cross are a symbol of Christ. They are in a modified Gothic form and represent the first three letters in the Greek word Jesus.

Symbols of Christ's sufferings are familiar. The CHALICE with a cross rising out of it symbolizes the agony of Gethsemane.[2] Used alone or with the wafer, the chalice suggests Holy Communion. The LANTERN, and BAG OF MONEY, are each used as symbols of the betrayal of Jesus by Judas.[3]

The CROWN OF THORNS tells of his physical suffering during the trial before Pilate and of the mockery of those soldiers who called him a king but did not believe in him.[4] The CRUCIFIX is a picture of Christ dying on the cross.

There are many *symbols of Christ*. This is to be expected. The FISH is probably the earliest. It reminds one of Christ's early association with the fisherman of Galilee and his calling them to "Follow me and I will make you fishers of men." [5] It became a secret sign among Christians in days of persecution. Outside of a Christian home, it meant that the Lord's Supper would be celebrated there that night. The Greek word for fish contains the first letters of the phrase, "Jesus

---

[2] Matthew 26: 39.
[3] John 18: 1-5, Luke 22:1-6, 47.
[4] John 19: 2-3.
[5] Matthew 4: 18-19.

Some Symbols Used in Worship

IHS - Iota Eta Sigma Chi Rho Chi Rho Alpha Omega Alpha Omega

Palm Branch Wheat Chalice and Wafer Grapes Olive Branch

Money Bag Lantern Gethsemane Chalice Thorn Crown and Nails

Latin Cross St. Andrew's Cross Maltese Cross Graded Cross

Christ, Son of God, Savior." This is the reason it was used as a sign among Christians.

The CANDLE represents Jesus as the Light of the World.[6] Two candles on the altar symbolize the two-fold nature of Christ, human and divine. The candles should always be lighted during a service of worship. A CROWN speaks of him as a king.[7] A LAMB suggests that he is "the Lamb of God that taketh away the sin of the world."[8] The head is sometimes shown with three rays, signifying divinity.

A figure representing the SUN symbolizes Christ as the "Sun of Righteousness."[9] IHS or IHC in Gothic letters stand for Christ. They are the first three letters in the Greek word for Jesus. They are sometimes enclosed in a circle which represents eternity. When rays are added, these symbmolize his glory.

Pictures of a SHEPHERD suggest Christ as the good Shepherd, who cares for his sheep.[10]

The CHI RHO is the first two letters of the Greek word Christ put in monogram form. The ALPHA and OMEGA are the first and last letters in the Greek alphabet and are a reminder of the reference to Christ in Revelations 1:8, "I am the Alpha and Omega." These letters are sometimes incorporated in the Chi Rho monogram by turning the X so that one arm is at right angles to the P and the Alpha and Omega are hung from the horizontal arms. The letters IX are the first letters of Jesus Christ in Greek.

---

[6] John 8:12.
[7] Luke 19:38.
[8] John 1:36.
[9] Malachi 4:2.
[10] John 10:11.

Some Symbols Used in Worship

The heads of WHEAT represent Christ as the Bread of Life,[11] since wheat is the grain from which bread is made.

Symbols of Christ's resurrection are used especially at Easter time. The plain CROSS is the most familiar and reminds us of both his death and resurrection. Christ died on a cross. The empty cross indicates that his death was not the final fact of his earthly ministry. He is a living Christ.

The BUTTERFLY is an interesting symbol of Christ's resurrection. The larval stage represents the mortal life. The chrysalis, which from all appearance is dead, symbolizes his death and burial. The last stage, in which the cocoon bursts open and the butterfly soars into the air, speaks of Christ coming forth out of the tomb on resurrection morning.

The PEACOCK is used to symbolize the resurrection because its new feathers, after molting, appear more brilliant. The BURSTING POMEGRANATE and the LILLY are also used to symbolize the resurrection. The bursting forth of life from that which appears to be dead is very appropriate to represent the resurrection of Christ.

Symbols of God tell of some particular power or attribute. The HAND with open palm, pointing downward from a cloud, indicates the creative power of God originating in his own glory and being.[12] Another symbol using the hand with fingers partially closed and small figures held in the closed fingers, represents the souls of the righteous held in the hand of God.[13] Sometimes the hand is used with the fingers pointing upward and placed so that they form the Greek letters which indicate Christ and so suggest the unity of the Father and Son.[14] The thought of benediction is expressed when the

---

[11] John 6: 35.
[12] Proverbs 1: 24.
[13] Psalm 139: 10 and Ecclesiastes 9: 1.
[14] John 10: 30.

thumb and two fingers point downward and two are folded up.

God's omnipresence is symbolized by the all-seeing EYE, suggested by such Scripture as 2 Chronicles 16:9. This figure is sometimes placed in an equilateral TRIANGLE whose three equal sides suggest the Trinity. It is sometimes seen above the altar. The CIRCLE is used to represent the eternal existence of God, for one cannot tell where a circle begins or ends.

The Holy Spirit is symbolized by a descending DOVE, suggested from the account of Christ's baptism.[15] The IRIS is sometimes used to symbolize the Holy Spirit and sometimes the Virgin Mary. The SEVEN TONGUED FLAME suggests the experience of Pentecost.[16] The SEVEN LAMPS are suggested by Revelation 4: 5.

The use of seven suggests the seven gifts of the Spirit, traditionally considered as power, riches, wisdom, strength, honor, glory, and blessing. Sometimes these are represented by seven doves with their heads pointing to a common center and enclosed in a circle.

The Trinity is symbolized by the EQUILATERAL TRIANGLE, by three INTERLINKING CIRCLES of equal size, and the TREFOIL which is the same figure with the overlapping parts cut out. They emphasize unity in the Trinity. There are several variations of this principle. Three fish are sometimes placed in a triangular form. This symbol is often found on baptismal fonts as a reminder that baptism is in the name of God, the Father, the Son and the Holy Spirit.

The use of the SHAMROCK to represent the Trinity originated in the legend concerning St. Patrick. It is said that he was talking to a pagan king one day and expressed belief

---

[15] Matthew 3: 16.
[16] Acts 2: 3.

in the doctrine of the Trinity. The king thought it absurd. St. Patrick reached down, plucked a twig of shamrock and used it as a symbol of one in three and three in one.

Other symbols are sometimes used in church buildings. The ROSE, which is probably most familiar as the rose window, is a symbol of the Messianic promise of Isaiah 35: 1, "the desert shall rejoice, and blossom as the rose." The BIBLE and THE LAMP are symbolic of the Word of God as a lamp unto our feet and a light upon our path.[17] The OLIVE BRANCH speaks of peace, concord, healing. The dove which Noah sent forth, brought back an olive twig which indicated to Noah that the waters were receding and the curse of the flood would be removed.[18]

The CROSS AND CROWN symbolize death and reward after death.[19] The PALM LEAVES suggest the Christian's reward when the race of life has been run.[20] The burning TORCH symbolizes witnessing activity, associated with the idea that Christians are the light of the world.[21] The pointed ARCH symbolizes aspiration and striving in spiritual growth. This is used in church architecture.

The SHIELD symbolizes trust.[22] The ANCHOR speaks of the hope we have in Christ.[23] The OX symbolizes patience, strength, sacrifice. The BURNING CENSER represents ascending prayer, worship and adoration. Clusters of GRAPES refer to the sacrament of Holy Communion. The LYRE suggests music. The CIRCLE OF LIGHT around the head of saints symbolizes sanctity.

---

[17] Psalm 119: 105.
[18] Genesis 8: 11.
[19] Revelation 2: 10.
[20] Revelation 7: 9.
[21] Matthew 5: 16.
[22] Ephesians 6: 16.
[23] Hebrews 6: 19.

Some Symbols Used in Worship

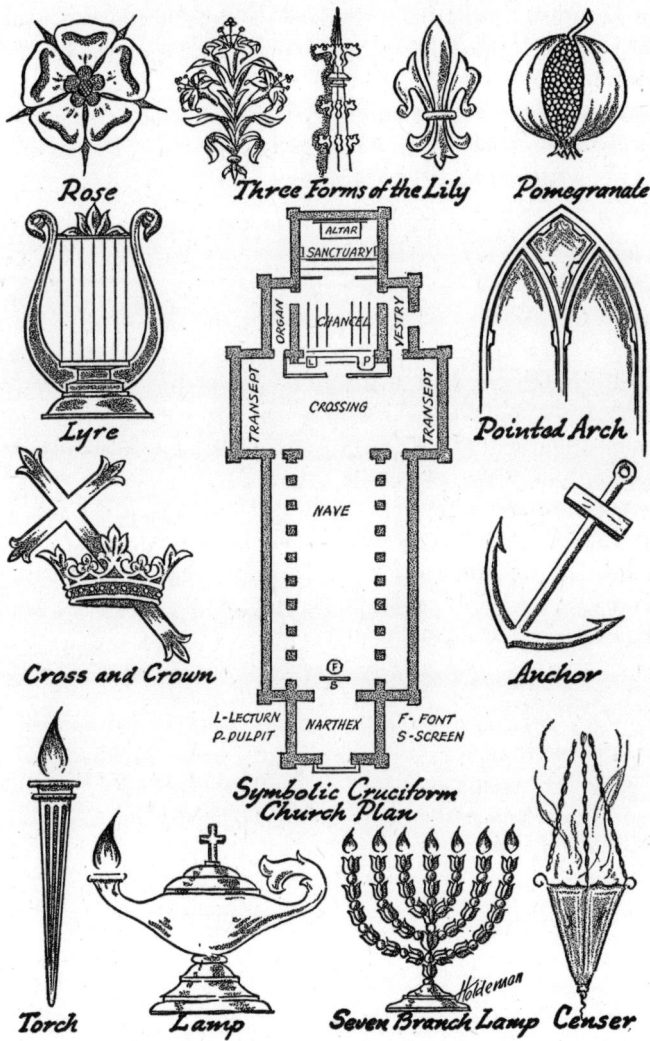

The STAR is symbolic of the star that guided the wise men to Jesus.[24] It is used at Christmas time and during the Epiphany season. The five-pointed star is associated with the Virgin Mary. The six-pointed star is a double triangle and is the star of David.[25] The seven-pointed star is symbolic of the seven gifts of the Holy Spirit.

Symbols for the apostles, each in the shape of a shield, came early. PETER is represented by two keys crossed over an inverted cross representing the apostle's sword. The keys recall the statement of Jesus concerning the keys of the kingdom.[26] The sword comes from Peter's use of it on the night of Christ's betrayal in an effort to defend him.[27] JOHN is represented by a serpent arising out of a chalice, said to have originated in the tradition that enemies attempted to poison him. An open Bible over a sword is on the shield that represents PAUL. He was a master at using the Word of God as the sword of the Spirit.[28] On the shield of STEPHEN are three stones and a coat, recalling his stoning while Saul held the coats of those who threw the stones.[29] JOHN THE BAPTIST is represented by a coarse coat on a shield, a reminder of the clothes he wore.[30]

The four evangelists are indicated by traditional symbols. MATTHEW is represented by a winged man. In his gospel, Christ is especially presented as the Son of Man. MARK is represented by a winged lion. His gospel puts emphasis upon the kingship of Christ. The power of the lion was associated

---

[24] Matthew 2: 2.
[25] Numbers 24: 17.
[26] Matthew 16: 19.
[27] Matthew 26: 51.
[28] Hebrews 4: 12; Ephesians 6: 17.
[29] Acts 7: 58.
[30] Matthew 3: 4.

Some Symbols Used in Worship

with royalty in ancient times. LUKE is represented by a winged ox. The ox was associated with sacrifice in the Old Testament and Luke points out the sacrificial aspect of Christ's life and ministry. JOHN is represented by an eagle. The gospel of St. John emphasizes the deity of Christ. Since the eagle soars higher than any other bird, it is a symbol of the gospel of John in which Christ's deity is emphasized.

Since there is a wide use of the *cruciform church* or a modification of it, its symbolism and the terms used with reference to it should be understood. It is certainly not necessary that we revert to Latin words, but it is important to know what they mean when they are used. One of the main principles of the Reformation was to put religion in the language of the people. The Bible was translated. Prayers and rituals were written in the language of the people.

By cruciform is meant a floor plan that resembles a cross. The sanctuary is the holy place where the altar stands. The chancel is in front of the sanctuary and is for the choir and clergy. In front of the chancel is the crossing, a space between the chancel and the place where the worshiping congregation assembles. This crossing or transept extends beyond the walls of the main building a little in order to give a modified form of the cross. The nave is the term used to speak of the main room where the worshipers assemble. The narthex is the vestibule or entrance hall. The term sanctuary is often used with reference to the entire room set apart for worship.

Symbols can be helpful if they are understood, but they are empty ornaments unless their significance is known.

Chapter 5

THE CHRISTIAN CALENDAR

ALONG with the development of symbols, a yearly cycle of doctrinal emphasis came to be associated with special seasons and days of the year. Colors for the altar coverings were prescribed in harmony with the spiritual meaning of these periods.

The Christian calendar developed out of the experience and life of the Church. It is not the product of one man or a group of men. It came out of the natural and normal desires of Christian people to celebrate and give recognition to certain events in Christ's life that were of special interest to them or that appeared to have significant meaning. The calendar provided a medium for the systematic teaching and the reviewing of the important happenings in the earthly life and ministry of our Lord. In this manner spiritual truths essential to Christian faith and life were kept before the people.

Proper celebration of special events require some preparation before hand. This led to the practice of designating a certain number of days or weeks leading up to the main events as seasons of spiritual preparation. In some instances a special day determines the nature of the period following. The general principle appears to have been that of accepting special days and then filling in between these days with appropriate and related seasons. Many of the names of these seasons carry the suffix, *tide*. This is Anglo-Saxon and means a time, a period or a season.

Selected Bible readings came next in the picture. Certain scriptural passages were designated as appropriate for reading during the various seasons of the church year. In this manner, over a long period of time, the Christian calendar developed as a yearly guide for worship. This followed the custom which prevailed in the synagogue of reading prescribed sections of the Law each Sabbath.

Churches differ in their use of the Christian calendar, but all churches use at least some parts of it. The use and emphasis vary according to theology, experience, background and the social customs of the group. The Protestant emphasis is not always the same as that of the Roman Church. In more recent years new elements have been added for Protestants, such as the Universal Week of Prayer and World-Wide Communion. Denominations have designated days for special emphasis to meet the spiritual needs of their people and promote Christian work.

Although each generation of Christians and every denomination should feel free to modify the traditional church calendar according to their needs, there is real value in retaining its general cycle which relates special periods to Christ and Christian experience. In this day of complex church organization and multiplicity of programs, special days are often scheduled arbitrarily with only a single need or objective in mind. These days are frequently for the promotion of a program or emphasis upon a special offering. This may get the money and make people acquainted with a program, but the spiritual significance of the church year may be missed.

Following the church calendar saves a pastor and his congregation from narrowness of interest and limited outlook, for during the year it calls attention to all of the major doctrines of the Christian faith. Denominations and local churches would do well to plan for special emphasis to harmonize with the seasons of the church calendar. This would meet the special needs and give the added advantage of spiritual significance to the event.

The Christian year begins four Sundays before Christmas with what is called the *Advent* season. The word is of Latin origin and means a coming. It is the period designated for preparing the mind and heart for a proper celebration of Christmas, the festival of Christ's birth. Violet or purple is the color for this period. For people of ancient times it suggested penitence, watching, fasting, self-examination, a looking within oneself, humility and repentance. This is the kind of spiritual preparation appropriate for a proper celebration of Christmas.

Christmastide includes the period from December 25 through January 5, taking in the two Sundays following Christmas. White is the color used because it symbolizes purity as reflected in the Virgin Mary and in the innocence of childhood. The emphasis for this period is the Incarnation of God in Jesus Christ.

The *Epiphany season* includes one to seven Sundays. The word is of Greek origin and means a showing forth. It was originally used with reference to the appearance or revelation of a supernatural being. In ancient times a Greek festival was held in certain places to celebrate the appearance of the gods. This festival was Christianized to be a reminder of the revelation of God in Christ to the Gentiles.

Epiphany is January 6, the day when the Wise Men were supposed to have visited Jesus. This is the beginning of the Epiphany season.

White is used on Epiphany and the first Sunday after Epiphany, but green is the color used during the rest of this period. It is the color of hope and growth. As trees and shrubs begin to put forth green leaves in the spring and we begin to look toward summer, so green is the color that represents hope and growth. The star is also used with Epiphany as a reminder of the star that guided the Wise Men to Jesus.

The emphasis during this period is on the manifestations of God in Christ. The miracles and parables of Jesus are among the listed readings. Christian missions are often emphasized during this period. Special events in the life of Christ to which attention is called during this season include the visit of the Wise Men,[1] his baptism,[2] the miracle of turning water into wine at the marriage feast in Cana[3] and the inquiry of the Greeks for Jesus.[4] These events have special significance as manifestations of Christ, each occurring at the beginning of a particular period in his earthly life.

Lent follows the Epiphany season and includes six Sundays. It is a forty day period (excluding Sundays) that begins with Ash Wednesday. This is the preparation period for Easter. Purple is used for altar and pulpit hangings because the Christian must search his own heart, and through repentance and discipline, prepare for the proper celebration of the resurrection of Christ. Sundays are excluded in counting the forty days because Sunday is the Lord's Day and is traditionally a festival day, a day of gladness, never of fasting.

The prominence of forty day periods in the Bible is responsible for the choice of forty days for Lent. Jesus was

---

[1] Mathew 2: 1-12.
[2] Matthew 3: 13-17.
[3] John 2: 1-11.
[4] John 12: 20-22.

in the wilderness of temptation for forty days,[5] the flood came out of forty days and nights of rain,[6] and the children of Israel wandered in the wilderness for forty years.[7]

Ash Wednesday is so named because of the ancient practice of opening the Lenten period with a service in which ashes were used as a sign of repentance "in sackcloth and ashes." The emphasis during Lent is on repentance, self-examination and spiritual renewal. Protestant churches often use this period for revivals and evangelistic meetings, visitation evangelism and decision days. Attention is given to the purification and cultivation of the inner life.

Passion Sunday is the second Sunday before Easter and opens Passion Week which is the second week preceding Easter. It calls attention to the redemptive suffering of Christ.

Holy Week includes Palm Sunday through Easter. *Palm Sunday* commemorates Christ's triumphant entry into Jerusalem.[8] Monday recalls Christ's cleansing of the Temple.[9] Tuesday finds him in conflict with his enemies.[10] There is no record of events for Wednesday. *Maundy Thursday* is the Thursday of Holy Week. The word means "order" and is used because it was on this night, when the Lord's Supper was instituted, Jesus washed the feet of his disciples and gave the new commandment, "That ye love one another.[11] Holy Communion is often observed on this day. If so, white should be used on the altar as in all communion services.

---

[5] Matthew 4: 1-11.
[6] Genesis 7: 4.
[7] Numbers 14: 33.
[8] Mathew 21: 1-11.
[9] Mark 11: 12-19.
[10] Mark 11: 20—13: 37.
[11] John 15: 12.

Good Friday is the day commemorating the crucifixion[12] and black is used on the altar, symbolizing death. A church that closely adheres to the ecclesiastical colors will also use black drapes for funerals and for days of national prayer in calamities. Good Friday services are appropriately centered in the crucifixion, and special attention is usually given to the seven statements which Jesus made while on the cross.[13]

Easter is the celebration of the resurrection of Christ and white is the ecclesiastical color. Easter is probably the oldest day in the church calendar, for the fact of Christ's resurrection has been central in Christian faith from the very beginning. This event was the turning point in the faith of the first disciples. It was the determining factor in fixing the first day of the week as the day for Christian worship, making the first day to be the Lord's Day.

Easter is not considered the close of Lent but the beginning of *Eastertide,* a period that runs from Easter to Ascension Day. White is used during this period, focusing attention upon the sinless glory of Christ. The joyful spirit of Easter should prevail during Eastertide.

Ascension Day recalls Christ's ascension and comes on a Thursday, forty days after Easter. It is the beginning of *Ascensiontide* and white is the color to be used on the altar, lectern and pulpit. The spirit of this season is that of victory and rejoicing. It marks the end of the first half of the Christian year, just as the ascension marks the end of Christ's personal ministry in the flesh.

Pentecost is the anniversary of the outpouring of the Holy Spirit upon the first disciples of Christ as recorded in Acts 2.

---

[12] Luke 23.
[13] Luke 23: 34, 43; John 19: 26; Mark 15: 34; John 19: 28, 30; Luke 23: 46.

Red is used on this Sunday because red represents fire, Christian zeal, the work and ministry of the Church. Red also symbolizes the blood of the martyrs upon which the Church was built. If only one color is to be used in a church the year around, it ought to be red, representing the continuous work and ministry of the Church.

Pentecost is one of the oldest days of the Christian calendar and is generally regarded as a celebration of the beginning of the Church. Appropriate readings for this period include those passages concerning the Holy Spirit and his work in and through the Church. The theme for the week is the Church and its work.

Pentecost is the beginning of *Whitsuntide* which lasts just seven days. The word came to be used because of the white robes worn by candidates received into the Church. Pentecost comes at the time when spring moves into summer and so represents the Church as moving out into the world in conquest. It is a period with emphasis upon the energizing power of the Holy Spirit.

This marks the beginning of the second half of the Church year. While the first six months center in the life and ministry of Christ, the second six months center in the Church and its work as continuing the ministry of our Lord. The general theme for the first half of the year is God's revelation of himself through Jesus Christ. The second half of the year follows the general theme of man's response to God in faith and service.

The *Trinity* season opens with Trinity Sunday, which is the Sunday following Pentecost. It is of English origin and spread from Canterbury. It follows Pentecost Sunday, indicating that all of the Persons in the Godhead have been revealed,

God the Father, the Son, and the Holy Spirit. The Trinity season is the longest period in the church calendar. It runs until Advent. Green is the color to be used, the color of growth and life. Some Protestant churches divide the Trinity season into two parts, by designating the period following the last Sunday in August as Kingdomtide.

The yearly cycle of the calendar is thus completed, showing God taking the initiative in providing for man's salvation and revealing this through the life and ministry of Jesus Christ, beginning with his birth and ending with his death, resurrection, and ascension. Then follows the descent of the Holy Spirit into the hearts of those who believe in the Son of God. The Church becomes a reality and the ministry of Christ is carried on by his followers. Man's salvation is dependent upon his response of faith to the divine revelation.

The Christian calendar provides a guide for preaching and worship that is helpful in giving a balanced emphasis to Christian doctrines and suggests Christian work appropriate for the seasons.

Chapter 6

ORDER AND RITUAL IN WORSHIP

WHEREVER two or more people come together for worship, there must be some accepted pattern and order to follow or there will be confusion. Some leadership must be given to the group.

In non-liturgical Protestant churches the minister has a great deal of freedom in planning the order of service to be used in his church. This is consistent with the freedom of Protestantism. It gives the minister opportunity for creating an order of service that can best meet the needs of his congregation and guide them in meaningful worship. It also makes it easy to adjust the order of worship to local custom and to the physical arrangements of the building.

This, however, places a great responsibility upon the minister. He is answerable for the service and its effect upon the people. This requires that he be familiar with the general principles of worship and know how to use them in creating orders of service that will guide the individual worshipers in sincere expressions of adoration and praise to God, and experience his Presence. The order of service should be planned as a chart to guide spiritual movement, beginning with the people as they are and leading them into the holy experience of communion with the Heavenly Father.

The effectiveness of a Protestant service of worship is largely determined by the man in the pulpit. It will be so from the moment he enters the chancel until he leaves it after the benediction. The very manner in which he enters, his dress, the expression on his face, the words he speaks, the way he speaks, and the general manner in which he conducts himself will all have an influence upon the congregation. He must use hymns, prayers, creed, Scripture, periods of silence, offering and sermon as means of guiding people in divine worship.

The three terms used with reference to the order of a worship service should be understood by all who are responsible for worship. We often use them rather loosely and sometimes interchangeably. An *order of service* refers specifically to the order in which the hymns, prayers, scriptures, and other parts of the service are arranged. This may vary according to time, circumstance, place and at the will of the minister in charge. *Liturgy* is the term usually used with reference to a fixed order of worship, often established by tradition. *Ritual* refers to fixed forms of worship, established by tradition or authority, for the observance of religious ordinances. The use of rituals has the advantage of giving the people a carefully prepared order of worship in the celebration of the sacraments and ordinances which combine the thought, experience and tradition of the Church, giving reverent dignity and meaning to the act.

The Protestant minister has the responsibility of using rituals and building an order of service for worship that will serve as a channel through which the individual can offer sincere spiritual worship to God and through which the Spirit of God can touch human life with redeeming grace. It is important for one to keep in mind the general movement of worship and the end toward which worship moves.

Worship begins in fixing the mind on God. For this reason the service of worship opens with a call to worship. This usually consists of words of Scripture spoken by the minister. Worship may begin with the congregation singing a hymn that exalts God. It may open quietly with the invocation which is a brief prayer that brings the congregation before God, requesting his Presence and guidance in the service. Devotional music properly selected and played, is very effective in creating an atmosphere of relaxed meditation which prepares the mind and heart for participation in worship. Worship can begin in a number of ways, but the important thing to remember is that whatever is done should direct the thoughts of the worshiper upon God. A prayer printed in the worship bulletin is helpful in fixing attention upon God and one's personal need of him.

The music, call to worship, invocation, and every part of the opening service must be selected with the purpose of directing the mind of the worshiper toward God. When people gather for worship, they come with the experiences and activities of the week on their minds. At the very beginning of the service, they must be led to turn their thoughts to God. He must be exalted above all as the holy Sovereign of the universe, Creator and Sustainer of all that exists.

The worshiper must then be led to judgment upon himself in the light of God's holiness. Hymns of the subjective type which direct the thoughts of the worshiper to his inward spiritual condition and need of a Savior are appropriate and helpful. Carefully selected scriptures, a period for silent prayer, a prepared prayer read in unison, and the pastoral prayer are aids in helping the worshiper in confession of sin. The assurance of forgiveness is brought to the worshiper through words of Scripture, a song or prayer.

The goal of worship is the dedication of life to God. Worship is not a program given by the minister for the entertainment of the people, but an experience through which he leads them. The service of worship is not a static thing but consists of spiritual movement, beginning where the people are and taking them into the holy place of personal fellowship with God where life is dedicated in service to him. Unless there is an experience of God and a dedication of life to him, worship has not truly taken place.

The sermon is very important in guiding people into proper dedication of the life to God.[1] It presents God's message to man and interprets it in terms of life. The sermon stands at a strategic and central place in Protestant worship.

An affirmation of faith is important in worship. There needs to be opportunity for people to declare their faith. Two generations ago our American Protestant churches did this largely through periods of individual personal testimony. The general practice now is to do it as a group, through the singing of hymns, the reciting of the Apostles' Creed or through the use of a passage of Scripture.

The offering is a means by which a part of one's possessions is dedicated to God for Christian service. The period for the offering should never be treated lightly but made meaningful, taken reverently by ushers, and properly dedicated with prayer by the minister. Bringing the collected offerings to the altar while the congregation is standing and singing the Doxology, and having it received by the minister who offers it to God in prayer, can be a means of meaningful worship.

The prayer after the sermon ought to beseech God, on behalf of the people, for grace and strength to respond to the challenge of the message. The hymn following the sermon

---

[1] Romans 12: 1.

ought to be one through which the people can express their renewed consecration in harmony with the sermon.

The benediction is the pronouncement of divine blessing upon the congregation of worshipers as they are ready to depart.

Some general observations: The *processional* at the beginning of the service reminds the worshipers that they are a part of that great throng of Christians of all ages who have come to the church to worship God and seek light on his ways. The *recessional* represents the Church going out into the world to live its faith and do the works of Christ. Every generation of Christians belong to a fellowship of believers that dates back to the time of the Apostles.

The *Gloria Patri* has been associated with the reading of the Scripture and especially with the Psalms. The *Doxology* is quite appropriately used with the dedication of offerings to God. *The Apostles' Creed* is one of the oldest and most familiar affirmations of faith. The Church has used it through many centuries.

Anthems, solos, and other special musical numbers should fit into the entire order of service and aid in worship rather than attract attention as ends in themselves.

Although the experience of worship may be analyzed in order to give guidance to a worshiping congregation, worship is not a series of separate experiences but a blending of them in such a pattern that the result is an awareness of God and a dedication of life to him. Some ministers will mark the pathway prominently and others will quietly lead their people over the same road without making them conscious of each step.

The *order of service* should be varied somewhat so that it does not become a deadening routine devoid of spirit. On the other hand there is an advantage in the people being able to follow a general procedure with which they are familiar. The purpose of an order of service is to serve as a guide and an aid to worship.

When praising God, we ought to stand. When praying we ought to assume a humble attitude. This means that as a general rule, the congregation will stand for singing those hymns which are acts of praise, be seated when singing those which are prayers, confession or supplications. The congregation will usually be seated with bowed heads or kneel for prayer, but stand with bowed heads for the invocation and benediction. Some congregations stand for the Scripture reading. This is appropriate for through the Bible, God is speaking to the people.

Chapter 7

LEADING OTHERS IN WORSHIP

THE responsibility of leading others in worship is one that none should accept lightly, for it means giving guidance in one of life's most holy acts and most sacred personal experiences. Such a task calls for careful preparation.

The responsibility is even greater in non-liturgical churches because the minister in charge must plan the complete order of service. Since the non-liturgical churches do not make extensive use of symbols and established liturgy in worship, the individual personality of the minister often has a strong influence in determining the effectiveness of the service. Even his dress, mannerism, voice and facial expression may help or hinder the group in the act of worship. What is true for the minister in conducting public worship is also true for the layman who is responsible for leading a group in a devotional period.

It is not an especially easy or simple task to guide a group of people into a real and meaningful experience of God, for God is neither visible to the human eye nor can he be touched by human hands. "God is a spirit, and they that worship him must worship in spirit and in truth."[1] We are so accustomed to visible things that it is sometimes very difficult for us to be aware of that which is invisible. Spiritual things must be spiritually perceived. The physical senses are not enough. This fact creates a difficulty for anyone who is responsible for leading a group of people in worship.

---

[1] John 4: 24.

The physical, mental and spiritual condition of the people has a great deal to do with determining the results of a worship service or a devotional period. If the majority of them have come with an attitude of indifference or have their minds so occupied that they do not cooperate with the leader in fixing their attention upon spiritual matters, it is difficult to guide them in meaningful worship. The leader must also take into consideration lack of knowledge of the Bible and of the great religious traditions of the Church.

It is the leader's responsibility to create a favorable atmosphere for worship and guide in an experience of worship. To do this, one will need to accept the people as they are and use many aids which are available to lead them into proper attitudes and appropriate expressions of worship. These must be carefully selected and properly used.

Music has always been associated with religion because it is a natural channel through which the soul can express itself. It will heal the troubled heart, lift up the depressed, cleanse the desires of the soul, and inspire men to high endeavor. It is the natural speech of worship, and can be very effective in unifying a group in its thinking and attitudes.

Music came into the Christian Church from the Hebrews. Hebrew poetry with its parallelism as noted in the Psalms is quite suitable for group singing. The Hebrews used the Psalms in their synagogues and the Christians followed their example. In addition to these, the Church has created other hymns and gospel songs that are expressive of Christian faith, hope and experience.

A choir school was established at Milan by St. Ambrose in the fourth century and another was established in Rome during the sixth century. The plain-song or chant was introduced. During the Dark Ages, church music became scholastic and was removed from the common people through the seclusion of the monasteries. With the coming of the Reformation, religious songs for congregational singing were written and often sung to some familiar folk tune. During the past century and a half, many hymns and gospel songs have been produced. Congregational singing is a very important part of Protestant worship.

The hymns at the opening of the service should be objective, turning the thoughts of the people to God. Other hymns and songs can be used to express confession, consecration, devotion, loyalty, or whatever fits into the order and purpose of the service. The words of the hymns should be appropriate, meaningful, and doctrinally sound. The tunes should be singable and reverent. The selections should be clearly and distinctly announced before the organist or pianist begins to play, clearly printed in an order of service or displayed on a hymn board, so that all can join in the singing.

Scripture selections should be made carefully and read effectively. Each word should be pronounced distinctly. The reading should be done slowly and loudly enough for the people to follow easily. It ought to be read before the time for public reading to check pronounciation of any words that may be unfamiliar. It should be read reverently for "all scripture is inspired by God"[2] and conveys a message from him.

It is not necessary that the Scripture lesson be on the same theme as that of the sermon unless it immediately precedes it. Since the order of service varies so much among churches, the place for the reading of the Scripture may vary. It should be placed where it will be most meaningful. Hymns and

---

[2] 2 Timothy 3: 16

prayers preceding it should lead up to it. Since the chief purposes of worship is communion with God and the Bible is God's Word, reading the Bible is a very holy act through which God speaks to the congregation.

The prayers should be in harmony with the spirit and purpose of the meeting. Public prayer is for the purpose of leading others in a presentation of themselves and their needs to God by guiding their thoughts in appropriate expression. It is different from private prayer in that one seeks to guide the thoughts of others in prayer. Because of this responsibility it is imperative that thought be given to what one will include in public prayer and the way it will be expressed. This does not necessarily call for written prayers nor for memorized prayers, but if careful thought is given to the prayer beforehand it will be more helpful.

Real prayer is not a matter of words but an aspiration of the soul. More important than giving prayer proper expression in words is the cultivating and maintaining of proper spiritual conditions and relationships from which true prayer can come. The quality of one's public prayers will depend much upon one's day by day spiritual life.

In keeping with the purpose of public prayer, one should use plural pronouns and make appropriate petitions which lift up and unify the needs and aspirations of the group. The leader must give thought to the needs of the group and the purpose of the meeting if he is to lead the group effectively in prayer. In addressing God, *Thou, Thy, Thine,* and *Thee* should be used.

The sermon or meditation, its length, type, and the way in which it is given, will depend upon many things. One must consider the size of the group, the purpose of the meeting, the place in which the group is assembled, the time allotted for the entire meeting, and other related factors. One would not give a formal address in a large auditorium in exactly the same manner one would speak to a dozen people in a small room.

Whatever message is given ought to be spoken distinctly, loud enough to be heard, and slowly enough that all can follow. Short and simply constructed sentences are more forceful than long ones. If the listener fails to catch the meaning of what one says and must attempt to reconstruct a statement in order to give more thought to it, he misses the trend of thought in what follows, and so may miss the main thought of the sermon.

The Christian message ought to be rooted in the Scripture. This may not necessarily always require a text but it does mean that what one says ought to be true to the teachings of the Bible. Interpretation of the Scripture is the major task and the high privilege of preaching, giving new light on old truths and unfolding the deeper meanings of passages as they are related to present day living. This is always helpful to both believers and to unbelievers.

Plan for every detail, in so far as possible, keeping in mind the specific purpose of the service. Include nothing to attract special attention to itself but plan all parts of the service so that the individuals in the group will be made aware of God and experience his Presence. Anything that fails to contribute toward this end ought to be omitted, no matter how good it may be in itself.

The physical surroundings should not be neglected. Although worship is essentially something of the spirit, external things associated with worship are important. We are spiritual beings but we are also physical. The body without the spirit would be dead. The spirit without the body would be a ghost. The whole person is involved in worship.

The one responsible for leadership in worship should see that the arrangements of the room are conducive to worship. The heat, light and ventilation of the room should be adjusted for comfort. Things which would detract from worship ought to be removed from the room. The minister of a church should check the sanctuary for these things. People will be easier to lead in worship if they are comfortably seated in a sanctuary that is properly lighted and ventilated.

The minister must prepare himself as well as the place and the order of service for worship. In so far as possible the body must be given sufficient rest the night before so that one can approach the hour of worship without weariness. God should have our best, not what is left over after we have expended most of our energy on our own interests. One must be mentally alert and spiritually sensitive to do a good job of leading others in worship. These qualities of life are cultivated through regular prayer, sincere faith, consistent effort to follow Christ, and humble devotion to him as Savior and Lord.

As one comes to the service, he must know what he is going to do and the way he is going to do it, but always be alert and responsive to any situation that may call for modification of plans. The chief purpose is not to conduct a service but to guide people in a spiritual experience. Do not be a slave to mechanics, but make them serve the purposes of the spirit.

The worshiper must prepare himself for worship. Such a high and holy act will be most meaningful only when proper preparation is made for it. Since one worships as a total person—mind, body, and spirit—the whole person must be considered. Preparation for worship should begin before the worshiper arrives at the place of worship.

Preparation for Sunday morning worship ought to begin on Saturday. Unless there is some good reason for doing otherwise, one should retire early enough to assure himself of a good night's rest so he can awaken refreshed on Sunday morning. The Saturday schedule should be planned and carried out with Sunday in mind. One should not leave anything for Sunday that can be done on Saturday, and neither should one plan activities for Saturday which consume more energy than a good night's rest can restore. Begin Saturday with the purpose of going to church the next day and go to bed in the evening with the same intention in mind. People who are in church on Sunday are there because they planned it that way.

The Sunday morning schedule ought to be planned so that one can leave home early enough to arrive at the place of worship on time. The strain and tension resulting from confusion and hurry is not conducive to meditation and worship. It is always beneficial if one can arrive at the church a few minutes before the service begins. These few minutes should be used to sit quietly and relaxed in the pew in meditation and silent prayer. The Christian symbols and other objects in the sanctuary will be helpful to direct one's attention to God and serve as a reminder of the purpose for which he came.

One can worship best if he is comfortably seated, not too crowded. Heavy and uncomfortable coats should be removed. The mind must be prepared for worship by fixing one's thoughts on God and one's personal need of him. The cross, the pulpit, the communion table and the altar are visible things that will help to direct thoughts toward God.

These are some of the things in which ministers should instruct their congregations to help them to discipline themselves for worship.

Chapter 8

WHAT IS APPROPRIATE IN WORSHIP?

PUBLIC worship in non-liturgical Protestant churches has no fixed pattern. The arrangement and order of the many details are left to the judgment of the minister. The devotional periods associated with small group meetings and led by laymen have no established order. The one who is responsible for leading others in a service of worship must not only know the meaning and principles of worship but must also have a sense of what is appropriate.

The purpose of this chapter is to give help to both ministers and laymen in cultivating a sense of what is appropriate in a service of worship.

Services of public worship should (1) direct the thoughts of the congregation toward God, (2) guide the individuals within the group in appropriate expressions of adoration and praise to God, (3) aid the worshipers in communion with God, and (4) lead them to a proper dedication of life to God. That which helps in accomplishing this is appropriate.

Anything which attracts special attention to itself for its own sake interrupts the worshiper in his thought of God and is not appropriate. A symbol whose meaning is not understood by the worshiper or a symbol that is not used in keeping with its significance, fails to serve as an aid in worship. It may even detract or confuse, and so is not appropriate. Every part of the worship service and everything associated with it must fit into its purpose and contribute toward its objective. The way a thing is done is often as important as doing it. Nothing should be done as an end in itself, but everything must contribute toward the purpose of the service.

Sufficient rules for every occasion cannot be made. The minister must cultivate a sense of what is appropriate and helpful for worship. He must develop the art of saying and doing the right thing even when there are no rules to guide him. Knowing some general principles is helpful but the minister must cultivate a spiritual sensitiveness through personal religious discipline and sincere dedication to his task. His own soul must be regularly nourished on the things of the Spirit. He must live close to people and be concerned for their spiritual welfare.

Candles are becoming common in non-liturgical churches. Their religious symbolism must be understood if they are to have any significance in worship. Unless they suggest some religious truth to the worshiping congregation they have value only as ornaments.

The association of candles with worship comes out of Christ's statement concerning himself, "I am the light of the world," [1] and his statement to his disciples, "Ye are the light of the world." [2] Unless the candle is burning there is no light. Therefore, if candles are used upon the altar or communion table, they should always be burning during the service of worship.

The candles should be lighted just before the beginning of the service, continue to burn during the entire service, and

---

[1] John 4: 12.
[2] Matthew 5: 14.

be extinguished after the benediction. The candlelighter usually wears a robe and carries a candlelighter or a lighted candle to use in lighting the candles on the altar or communion table. If the candles are lighted by an usher, no robe is necessary. Some ministers prefer to extinguish the lighted candles after they have spoken the benediction.

A single candle on either side of a cross is the usual arrangement in the Protestant church. The candles should never be higher than the cross. The one on the left stands for Christ in his humanity and for the Gospels that record the important events of his earthly ministry. The candle on the right represents Christ's deity and the Epistles which exalt him as divine Savior and Lord. Both symbolize Christ as the Light of the world.

When reciting the Apostles' Creed, the congregation should stand. This is an affirmation of faith in which the individual worshipers give testimony of their personal belief in God, the Father, the Son, and the Holy Spirit.

Since there is a variation in the form of the Apostles' Creed as used by the churches, the pastor should acquaint his congregation with the form to be used so that there will be uniformity when it is spoken. This is easy to do if printed worship bulletins are used.

The Doxology and Gloria Patri are hymns of praise. The congregation should stand while singing them. Heads should be up, not bowed, and eyes should be open. Neither of these are prayer hymns. The Doxology is often used in connection with the dedication of the offering. The Gloria Patri is traditionally associated with the reading of the Scripture, especially the Psalms. It properly follows the reading of Scripture.

The congregation should always stand for the singing of hymns of praise. These hymns express adoration and praise to God. Standing is a way of showing respect and reverence toward God. Hymns which are prayers, meditative or subjective in thought, should be sung with the congregation seated. The people should stand for the closing hymn which ought to be one expressing appropriate response to the sermon.

Prayers are important in worship. The invocation comes at the beginning of the service and is a short prayer in which God is petitioned to be present and give guidance to the service. The congregation should be standing with bowed heads for this prayer.

The pastoral prayer is one made by the minister on behalf of the congregation. It usually comes in the earlier part of the service before the sermon. In it, the minister voices the petitions of the people, guiding and expressing their thoughts through his words. A minister must know the people of his parish, be acquainted with their problems, and be concerned with their spiritual welfare if he is to be effective in pastoral prayer. He should give some thought to this prayer beforehand in order to include in it those petitions which bring together the needs of the entire congregation. The same is true where the chief prayer comes after the sermon.

Prayer is appropriately followed by a response sung by the choir or by the congregation, to express the congregation's response to the prayer. Such response was formerly more often vocalized in non-liturgical churches by spontaneous "Amens" spoken by individuals of the congregation.

The congregation will usually be kneeling or seated with bowed heads for the pastoral prayer. This position expresses petition, humility and surrender.

The benediction is a word of blessing spoken by the minister to the worshipers before their departure. The congregation should stand with heads reverently bowed. Symbolic of the blessing given, the minister lifts up his hands over the people while he speaks the words of benediction.

Although prayer is sometimes spoken at the close of a service of worship, the benediction itself is not a prayer. It is a pronouncement of blessing. In it the minister is speaking for God to the people, pronouncing divine blessing upon them. It is proper, therefore, for him to speak the words of the benediction with his eyes open. In the regular worship service it is usually better to have prayer follow the sermon and let the benediction be given alone at the conclusion of the service.

The open chancel sanctuary should be used in keeping with its symbolism.

If the chancel rail has a gate across the central aisle this should be closed when no service is being conducted in the sanctuary. When it is time to begin the service of worship, two ushers should walk reverently down the center aisle, open the gates, and stand there for the processional of choir and clergy. They should then retire to the rear of the room. At the close of the service they should come forward and stand, one on either side of the gate, while choir and clergy leave the chancel. They should then close gates and follow in the recessional.

Where there is both a lectern and pulpit, no one should enter the pulpit but the minister, and he should go into it only for the preaching of the sermon. All other acts associated with the conduct of the service should take place at the lectern, at the altar or at the communion table. The pulpit is to be reserved for the sermon, emphasizing its important and significant place in worship. If Sunday school assemblies or other types of meetings are held in the sanctuary, they should be conducted from the lectern or from a table provided for that purpose, never from the pulpit.

In dedicating the offering it should be received by the minister from the ushers and placed upon the communion table or altar with a prayer in which the gifts of the people are presented to God. It is proper for the prayer to be spoken by the minister while he faces the communion table or altar, for he is thus taking his place with the congregation in presenting his gifts as well as theirs. Some prefer to place the offering plates on a stand at the side.

Empty offering plates should never be kept on the altar or communion table, for they are only plates in which the offering is placed. It is the offering that has religious significance, representing the dedication of life to God. The money in the offering plates represent human energy, thought, time and skill exchanged for coin and currency, and in this form offered to God.

The minister's dress is not specified by non-liturgical churches, but this does not mean it is unimportant. Every minister should give careful attention to what he wears when conducting divine worship.

The academic or Geneva style robe is worn by Protestant ministers in either the open chancel or pulpit-centered church. The closed style Geneva robe is probably the more preferable of the two, although they are very similar. This is distinctive of the Protestant clergy and is a definite contrast from the priestly dress of the Roman clergy. The Protestant minister is a preacher, a student and an interpreter of the Word of God to men. As a Bible scholar, he stands in the line of the scribes who were the scholars and teachers of Scripture in Old Testament times. As a preacher of the gospel he stands in the heroic line of the Old Testament prophets and the Apostles who called people to repentance and proclaimed God's redeeming grace.

If the church choir is robed, the minister should wear a robe. If the sanctuary has an open chancel arrangement the choir and the minister should be robed. Regardless of the color of the robes worn by the choir, the minister should wear black. In extremely warm climates or during excessive heat of summer months, some approve a white robe for the minister.

If the minister wears a stole over his robe, the color of the stole should correspond to the seasonal color of the church calendar. The stole is a symbol of the yoke. It is worn when conducting public worship, signifying that the minister is doing the work of Christ. A yoke is that special shaped piece of wood which is worn on the neck and shoulders of oxen to enable two of them to work together in pulling a wagon or a plow. A stole therefore symbolizes being in service, harnessed to Christ and doing his work under his leadership. The stole is also considered a symbol of ordination.

Black attracts no attention to itself and becomes a means of submerging the individual personality and dress of the minister so that the congregation is made less conscious of the man and more conscious of what he says. This is an advantage in worship, for it is important that the worshiper be more conscious of God than of men. The minister's chief purpose is to exalt God, and to make the congregation aware of God and of his presence. The sincere minister never exalts himself but endeavors to keep himself in the background. "We preach not ourselves, but Christ Jesus the Lord." [3]

If the minister prefers to wear a regular suit in the pulpit-centered church, black is preferable. During months of excessive heat a light weight and light color suit is permissable but it should be conservative so as not to attract special attention to itself. The necktie should be appropriate. Pencils and fountain pens should be kept out of the outside coat pocket. Clothes should be clean and pressed. Shoes should be shined. A white shirt is preferable for pulpit dress, never a colored one. Although some may prefer to wear stripped trousers and a cutaway coat, this has no religious significance. A regular dark business suit or double-breasted suit is appropriate for use in the pulpit-centered church. One should dress in a manner that will not attract special attention to oneself, for the chief purpose of the minister is to make people aware of God.

Some Protestant ministers of the non-liturgical churches prefer to wear the distinctive dress associated with the clergy. This distinguishes them as ministers wherever they go and often gives opportunity to witness for Christ and minister in his name on occasions in which it would not otherwise be so. It is a professional dress, indicating that he is on duty, ready for a spiritual ministry to people, just as the soldier's uniform or the surgeon's white coat represents the man on duty. When such distinctive dress is worn by the Protestant minister the vest usually has a wider opening at the collar than that worn by the Roman clergy.

The minister must cultivate a sense of what is appropriate for the occasion. His dress in the pulpit should never attract

---

[3] II Corinthians 4: 5.

special attention to itself, either because of style or colors. He must dress and act so as to make people as little conscious of himself as is possible in order that what he says and does may make them more conscious of God. People should depart from the hour of worship more aware of having been in the presence of God than of having seen a man on a platform.

PART THREE

THE USE OF RITUALS

Chapter 9

BAPTISM

BAPTISM from the earliest times has been considered the initiatory rite signifying one's entrance into the fellowship of the Church. It is an outward act that represents an inward and spiritual relationship based upon one's acceptance of Jesus Christ as Savior and Lord. It was practiced by the Church from the very beginning.[1]

Baptism was not a new thing introduced by the Church. It was regularly required of Jewish converts. The Jewish baptism was a ceremonial washing, a sign of purification from the former way of living. Since water is the element most naturally used for the cleansing of the body, it is not surprising to find it associated with religious faith as a symbol of cleansing from old ways of living and the beginning of a new life.

The baptism of John the Baptist, however, was more than a symbol of ceremonial purification. It was a baptism of repentance, a confession of sin and an acknowledgment of the need of moral cleansing.[2] It was a sign of moral purification. John demanded that even Jews who were already ceremonially pure should be baptized.

John's baptism was not the same as Christian baptism. It symbolized repentance, the preparation to receive salvation,

---
[1] John 4: 1, 2; I Corinthians 1: 13-16; Galatians 3: 27.
[2] Matthew 3: 5-11.

but not entrance into the kingdom of God.[3] Even those who had been baptized by John were required by the Church to be baptized again.[4]

Christian baptism is more than a ceremonial washing. It is more than a preparation for salvation. It symbolizes the beginning of Christian discipleship. As an outward act it represents the spiritual experience of remission of sin,[5] regeneration,[6] union with Christ,[7] and is associated with membership in the Church.[8]

Baptism implies that those who receive this sacrament have experienced the cleansing of the Holy Spirit. Just as water cleanses the body, so God in Christ cleanses the soul from sin by the Holy Spirit, freeing a man from the dominating power of sin and initiating the beginnings of a new life. This new life is associated with and received through Christ. Salvation is a gift from God, appropriated through faith in Christ that unites the believer to him as Savior and Lord. Baptism is the outward and visible sign of an inward and spiritual cleansing of the soul. This spiritual cleansing is so complete that it is essentially a spiritual rebirth. Baptism is not the agent but the sign of this new birth. It is also an act through which the individual publicly declares his faith and gives witness to spiritual regeneration.

Infant baptism is based upon the belief that children of believing parents are within the church fellowship and that there can be a conscious, personal appropriation of the sacrament if the child is given proper guidance and teaching.

---

[3] Luke 1: 17.
[4] Acts 19: 1-5.
[5] Acts 22: 12-16; Hebrews 10: 22.
[6] John 3: 5; Titus 3: 5.
[7] Galatians 3: 27; Romans 6: 3-14.
[8] Acts 2: 41.

When parents present their children for baptism, they take vows to teach them the Christian way of life, nurture them in the Church, pray with them, teach them to pray, and guide them in the acceptance of Christ as their personal Savior. This is to imply that no individual life is a totally isolated and independent existence but is influenced by others, and that conscious faith in God can develop under the proper influence. It is a fact that one does come to trust a thing or an individual through many and varied influences. Our trust in God comes in the same way, not on our own initiative but through the impact of the Holy Spirit upon our lives through the example and testimony of others. It is a gift of God.

Infant baptism is an act in which the parents commit the child to Christ and pledge their consecrated efforts to guide the child through life's experiences in such a manner that he will come to a conscious and intelligent faith in Christ that entrusts life to him as Savior and Lord.

The different forms of baptism symbolize different aspects or viewpoints of spiritual regeneration. Immersion is an illustration of the believer's identification with Jesus Christ in his death, burial, and resurrection to a new way of living. Sprinkling is a reminder of the spiritual cleansing by the Holy Spirit which takes place through our faith in Jesus Christ and commitment of life to him.

Although pouring is not so generally practiced, it reminds one of the outpouring of the Holy Spirit upon the believers at Pentecost and is an outward act that symbolizes God's gift of the Spirit to all believers.

The baptismal service should be carefully planned by the minister and explained to the persons to be baptized, so that it can be reverently carried out without confusion.

If baptism is to be by immersion, arrangements must be made to have the baptistry filled with water and ready at the proper time. Unless it is during the summer, it will be desirable to have the water warmed. Dressing room facilities must be provided. If the baptistry is in the sanctuary, the baptism can come at the close of the worship service. The congregation can sing an appropriate hymn while the minister and the candidates for baptism make the proper change of clothes. If the baptistry is not in the sanctuary or an outdoor service is planned at a lake or a stream of running water, then a separate service must be arranged.

The minister should lead the candidate into the water when the time comes for the individual to be baptized. In the act of immersion it will often be found helpful to hold a folded handkerchief over the candidate's nose and mouth, and have the candidate place his hands on the minister's hand. The minister's other arm should be placed around the shoulders of the candidate, and the candidate should lay back in the minister's arm as he lowers his arm under the water. This makes for both ease and safety in holding the candidate as his body is lowered into the water and raised up again.

Except where custom or church rule instructs differently, the candidate is usually immersed backwards. If the candidate is much taller than the minister, it will be easier to have the candidate kneel in the water and lie back in the minister's arm. The minister then lowers his arm under the water until the face of the candidate is covered. As soon as his face goes beneath the surface of the water, the minister will raise him up.

Where baptism is to be done by sprinkling, a baptismal bowl or an appropriate vessel must be provided and filled with water. The minister should handle the bowl carefully so as to avoid any accidental spilling of the water. If a baptismal font is provided he merely has to arrange to have it filled.

In the act of sprinkling, the minister dips his hand into the water and sprinkles it upon the head of the candidate. Although the trinitarian formula is used in baptism, in the name of God, the Father, the Son and the Holy Spirit, this does not indicate three baptisms and the minister should dip his hand into the water only once for each candidate.

The candidate to be baptized by sprinkling should kneel at the chancel rail or at the place provided beside the baptismal font. If a woman candidate should appear at the chancel wearing a hat, the minister will quietly instruct her to remove it. Never embarrass anyone in such a situation or make an individual feel that a serious mistake has been made. Many women do not feel "right" in appearing at a service of worship without a hat.

When pouring is to be the method of baptism, the procedure should be about the same as that for immersion except that the candidate will stand or kneel in the water, while water is poured over his head.

The baptismal ritual provided by the Church should be used by the minister. At the appointed time in the service, the candidates shall be called forward by name or the minister can have an understanding with them to come at the announcement of the service of baptism.

When the candidates have presented themselves at the chancel of the church or at the designated place of baptism, the minister shall proceed to read the proper ritual. If there are both adults and small children to be baptized at the same service, it will be more effective for the minister to combine the essential parts of the ritual designed for use with children and the one designated for adults. This can be done by making a careful study of the two rituals to discover the parts which are common to both and those parts which are distinctive to each.

The ritual should be read slowly and reverently. The words should be spoken distinctly. The minister should make himself familiar with the ritual so that it can be followed without confusion. The places where the minister must speak the words appropriate to the group or individual candidate must be carefully observed.

The headings at the different sections of the ritual are to give guidance to the minister so he may act appropriately. They are not to be read aloud, but the congregation and the candidates should be able to tell when the minister is talking to them. When the prayers are made, all should bow their heads.

Chapter 10

THE LORD'S SUPPER

THE Lord's Supper or Holy Communion is that distinctive rite of Christian worship established by our Lord Jesus Christ upon the eve of his crucifixion and death. In this ceremony the worshiper religiously partakes of bread and wine that has been presented before God in thankful memorial of Christ's sacrificial death through the sacramental blessing. He accepts these elements as the communion of Christ's body and blood.

From the very early days of the Church the Lord's Supper has been regularly celebrated. It was at the center of the worship and fellowship of the early Christians. The records indicate that it was celebrated each Lord's Day. In the period following the death of the Apostles when public services of Christian worship became a general practice, the celebration of the Supper was given a central place in worship. The non-Christians were dismissed after the sermon while only the believers remained for Holy Communion. In some places the Supper was held in the evening.

The institution of the Lord's Supper is told in the Gospels. Jesus arranged for the celebration of the Passover with his Apostles in an upper room at a friend's house. After the meal he took bread from the table, gave thanks, and blessed it. The bread thus became a thank offering to God and was set apart for a holy purpose. He then broke the loaf of bread, gave it to the disciples and told them to eat it, saying,

"This is my body given for you."[1] He did the same thing with the cup, using similar words.[2]

The language of the Lord's Supper is sacrificial. The elements which are used are suggestive of sacrifice. They are associated with the old Jewish system of worship.[3] The crushing of the grapes to extract the juice and the grinding of the grain into flour for making bread suggests the suffering of our Lord in his sacrificial giving of himself.

Some of the Lord's miracles and discourses appear to have been object-lessons to prepare his disciples for this moment. At least they help us to understand some of the deeper meanings of the Lord's Supper. For example, after feeding the five thousand, Jesus talked about himself as the Bread of Life and said that men must eat his flesh and drink his blood if they are to share in eternal life.[4]

A ritual for the celebration of the Lord's Supper developed early in the history of the Church. It opened with a summons for the people to "Lift up their hearts." This was followed with a prayer of thanksgiving and praise to God for all the blessings of creation and the redemption which he brought about through the Incarnation. The Greek word used to designate this prayer was Eucharist, derived from *eucharistia,* meaning "giving of thanks." This same word was often used by the people in referring to the entire service, probably because it came at the beginning. It is so used today by some churches.

This prayer was followed by reading the account of the Last Supper as given in the Gospels, or the telling of the story

---
[1] Luke 22: 19.
[2] Luke 22: 20.
[3] Exodus 29: 2, 40.
[4] John 6: 53.

if scriptures were not available. The elements were then set apart as a memorial to Christ through humble prayer in which God was asked to hallow the bread and wine so set apart, in order that the act of partaking of these elements might be a spiritual communion of the body and blood of Christ for the remission of sin and the giving of eternal life. The bread and wine were then reverently received.

The Protestant emphasis on the Lord's Supper is different from that of the Roman Catholic Church. In 1215 A. D. Pope Innocent III, at the Lateran Council, established the doctrine of transubstantiation as the official belief of the Roman Catholic Church regarding the Lord's Supper. This doctrine declares that by the word of the priest the bread and the wine set apart and used in celebrating the Lord's Supper are transformed into the real body and blood of Christ. The word transubstantiation is of Latin origin combining the words meaning "across" and "substance" to give the idea of one substance being changed into another. This has been the doctrine of the Roman Church ever since.

According to this doctrine, the body and blood of Christ replace the substance of the bread and wine, although hidden from observation under the appearance of the elements. The whole Christ is present in each of the elements, so it is not necessary to commune in both forms. Sacrifice becomes the central thought as the bread and wine on the altar become a sin offering, offered by the priest on behalf of those who are present and even for the dead in purgatory. The Roman Church refers to the Lord's Supper as the mass.

The Protestant Church rejects the Roman Catholic doctrine of transubstantiation and its implications. The celebration of the Lord's Supper is not a sacrificial offering of Christ as a sin offering but is a memorial of his giving of himself as our sin offering. Celebration of the Lord's supper is an act done in memory of Christ's death through which we express our faith in his death as a redemptive act.

The celebration of the Lord's Supper is a memorial service, but it is more than a memorial. It is a symbol of Christ's death, but it is more than a symbol. It is an agency of divine grace by which the believer has spiritual fellowship with Christ through faith.

The blessing of the elements is an act of consecration in which they are set apart through prayer and the repetition of the words of institution. Protestants do not believe that a miracle changing the substance of the elements into the real body and blood of Christ takes place, but look upon it as solemn declaration that this bread and wine is separated from common use to be devoted to this special spiritual service. This is done in the belief that Christ's presence will be associated with that bread and wine as in the first communion, so that the individual spiritually feeds on Christ.

The Lord's Supper is a sacrament. The word means an outward and visible ceremony of the Church which serves as a sign of the inward and invisible mercy and love of God toward the believer. The sacramental act is complete in the consecration, distribution, and reception of the elements.

The sacrament bestows no blessing by the mere act of its mechanical performance. Faith is esential for the worshiper to experience the blessings of spiritual communion with Christ and witness to his personal spiritual union with him.

Holy Communion is the most complete symbol of our religious faith. It is an act in which the minister, acting in Christ's name, gives to the worshiper that which is symbolic of Christ giving himself in death. As the worshiper receives the elements of the sacrament, it is symbolic of his acceptance of the divine redemptive grace which alone can save from sin. Salvation is not something earned or obtained by a bargain with God. It is a gift from God.

The forgiveness of sin that establishes right relationship with God can never be purchased. It must always originate in the merciful heart of the One who has been sinned against. Forgiveness of sins must come out of the love and mercy of God. A sinner cannot forgive himself. Forgiveness can be accepted only as a gift of God's mercy and love. "To as many as received him, to them gave he the power to become the sons of God." [5]

The service of Holy Communion should be carefully planned and every part of it should be conducted reverently. There should be dignity but not stiffness, order but not empty formality. Many a Protestant communion service, hampered by an attempt to be orderly and impressive, actually results in a cold and mechanical performance of a ritual that should warm the heart and quicken the spirit of both the minister and his people. When a minister develops an inner tension by being unusually anxious about the mechanical movement of a service, the worshipers will become more aware of the physical than of the spiritual, and this defeats the very purpose of the Lord's Supper. The service ought to move easily and orderly, in harmony with the spirit of our Protestant faith which emphasizes the reality of Christian experience. The Lord's Supper is not a sacrifice offered on behalf of the people but an act of holy communion with God through faith in Jesus Christ. Communion means a conscious, personal and spiritual fellowship.

---

[5] John 1: 12.

The worshipers should be properly instructed throughout the service, either through a printed bulletin placed in their hands or through words spoken by the minister as the service proceeds. Giving oral instructions during the service often puts people more at ease than for them to be required to follow a printed bulletin. It is difficult to include sufficient printed instructions for people who are not regularly in the local service. Verbal direction for proper participation can be given without detracting from the service.

The ritual provided by one's own denomination should be used, adjusted to the local situation when necessary. The minister should take care that all of the essentials are included whenever the ritual is shortened. There should always be the blessing and words of institution which set apart the elements, the distribution, and the reception of the elements. The prayers, scriptures, hymns, and the sermon should help prepare and guide the minds and hearts of the worshipers in spiritual communion with the Redeemer.

The Protestant clergyman has a good deal of freedom in the use of rituals but it should be remembered that proper use of the accepted rituals of the church in which one ministers is a unifying force for Christian fellowship. Details may vary but the general pattern should be followed. Changes should be made in the ritual only for valid reasons. Minor details, however, may be left to the discretion of the minister. In most non-liturgical churches the pastor and his congregation may determine whether the sacrament is to be celebrated once a month or once every three months, whether it will be celebrated at the altar or while the people remain in the pews, how the distribution is to take place, the length of the service, and similar matters.

When the communicants come to the altar, it is preferable that they kneel and the minister himself distribute the elements. When it is received in the pews, he will need to select others to help with the distribution. When this is done, a plan of distribution must be carefully worked out and each person must know just what he is to do. The serving of the elements should take place as quietly and orderly as possible, but no tip-toeing or making of signs. Handle the elements reverently but naturally.

If the celebration of the Lord's Supper is to be truly a holy communion between the worshipers and the heavenly Father, the minister must give attention to creating the proper atmosphere in which it is possible for such spiritual communion to take place. The form and order of the service will have much to do with this, but more than form is needed. The minister must plan and conduct the service with the purpose of creating a spiritual atmosphere that will make it easy for the individuals in the congregation to give appropriate response to the celebration of the sacrament. The success of such efforts will depend much upon the spiritual sensitiveness of the minister.

The minister must be spiritually prepared for the service of Holy Communion. A part of this preparation will come out of his general spiritual attitudes and the quality of his devotional life. This in turn will depend upon study and prayer habits, consecration, personal righteousness, and other factors that determine character. It will also depend upon the special personal preparation which he makes for the specific service.

There should be thoughtful planning for the mechanics of the service. Consideration should be given to every phase of it, keeping in mind the people who make up the congregation. It should be the subject of prayer. No detail should be neglected.

The minister should go into the service with his mind fixed on the purpose of this high and holy celebration. He is a humble servant of God, ministering in the name of Christ. People must be made more conscious of Christ than of him. They must be reminded of their personal need of Christ's redemption from sin and be guided in making proper response to the spiritual significance of the sacramental act of Holy Communion.

Chapter 11

THE RECEPTION OF CHURCH MEMBERS

RECEPTION into the membership of a church ought to be a meaningful experience. Joining a church is not the same thing as joining a civic club or lodge. It is a confession of one's faith in Jesus Christ as Savior and Lord, and an expression of one's purpose to unite with other Christians in an organized fellowship for worship and service.

The Church had its beginning in the earthly ministry of Jesus. Those who responded to the call of discipleship became the first members of this fellowship which centers in Christ.

When our Lord was with his disciples in Caesarea Philippi he asked them what they thought of him. Peter responded by witnessing to the faith of the group, saying "Thou art the Christ, the Son of the living God. And Jesus answered and said unto him, Blessed art thou, Simon Bar-Jonah: for flesh and blood hath not revealed it unto thee, but my Father who is in heaven. And I say also unto thee that thou art Peter, and upon this rock I will build my church.[1]

The word used by Jesus which we translate church is one whose root indicates "a call." It was the same word used to designate the democratic Greek city assembly. When city business required a meeting of the citizens, a summons was issued and town criers went through the streets, calling peo-

---
[1] Matthew 16: 16-18.

ple to assemble at the square. Those who assembled in response to this call were the *ekklesia*. The word literally means, "those who have responded to the call." This is the word Jesus used when talking to the disciples at Caesarea Philippi, declaring that he would build his church (ekklesia) upon the foundation he had laid in the Apostles.

Through the use of this word, it is clear that one becomes a member of this spiritual fellowship through proper response to Christ's call to discipleship. The required response is a faith in Jesus Christ that commits life to him as Savior and Lord. Such faith brings life into spiritual union with Christ in a way in which he becomes the very life of the believer. "Christ liveth in me." [2]

This union of the believer with Christ is the central idea in the reference to the Church as the Body of Christ. He is said to be the head. This does not mean that believers are one part of the Church and Christ is another, but that there is a oneness of the believer with Christ. The head controls the body. Believers are under Christ's control through faith that surrenders life to him. What happens to the head happens to the body. Our redemption from sin rests not upon our faith but upon the fact of our being united with Christ as a result of our faith. The New Testament repeatedly speaks of the believer as being in Christ. Our hope is in Christ, not what we believe about him. Since the believer is in Christ, what happens to Christ happens to the believer, for he is the head of the body, the first fruits of the resurrection. As Christ died and arose to new life, so the follower of Christ must become dead to sin and be resurrected to new life. As dead things do not respond, so the believer must not be responsive

---

[2] Galatians 2: 20.

THE RECEPTION OF CHURCH MEMBERS 113

to sin. Life's direction must be taken from Christ, not from human desires and impulses.

Christ's earthly body was the visible means through which he had contact with the world. The Church is Christ's body, the visible organism that puts the unseen Christ in contact with the world today. As his body, the Church is animated by his Spirit. It is the agency through which his gospel is proclaimed and his life is made known. In order that his work might be done, the members are endowed with different gifts, just as members of the human body are made to serve different needs. Although gifts differ they are of the same spirit and for the same purpose—service in Christ's name. None are to esteem themselves above others.[3]

The Church expresses itself in and through units of organized believers who meet for worship and fellowship, and unite in Christian service. This is the visible church. The local groups are organized into denominations, each with its own formal confession of faith and traditional ways of doing things. An individual Christian should unite with that local group of Christians which seems to best express his personal faith, offers a fellowship most beneficial to himself, and provides a means through which his Christian faith can be expressed in Christian service.

In becoming a member of a local church one publicly declares his response to Christ's call to discipleship. One does not become a member of a church by declaring faith in the group, but by confessing faith in Christ as Savior and Lord. Membership in a church is based upon a faith relationship with Christ, and through this faith in him there is fellowship with others whose faith likewise centers in him.

---
[3] Romans 12.

The Church is basically a spiritual fellowship and so is not limited by time and space. It includes all believers in all ages. Since this fellowship is not dependent upon physical conditions or relationships, physical changes and differences do not alter it. Death does not destroy this fellowship. Our generation stands in the shadow of a great "cloud of witnesses."[4] The church yard which was used as the burial grounds in earlier days was a recognition of the continuance of this fellowship beyond the land of the living. Memorials in church buildings today are reminders of saints who have moved to the land beyond.

Differences in color or culture are no barriers to this Christian fellowship because this is a fellowship with one another based upon the individual's fellowship with Christ. The Church includes people of all races and nations of mankind.

Reception into the membership of a local church is based upon the evidence given by the individual that he has become a part of the spiritual and invisible Church through proper faith in Jesus Christ. In the ritual of reception into membership, the applicant gives this evidence by answering questions. The minister should discuss and explain these questions with the individual beforehand so that he understands the meaning and relationship of the questions to Christian faith and living.

It is proper that faith in the Bible be affirmed because it is the Word of God, and upon the message of this book our faith rests. Confession of Jesus Christ as Saviour and Lord is important because this is the central fact of the Christian faith. Before a congregation accepts an individual into membership, it has a right to require of the applicant some state-

---

[4] Hebrews 12: 1.

ment of purpose regarding his renouncing of sinful ways, commitment to follow Christ and his purpose to make use of the various means of grace provided for Christian growth and fellowship. Faithful attendance at the services of the church, regular reading of the Bible, daily prayer, and sharing in the celebration of Holy Communion are necessary if church membership is to be meaningful.

Each member of the congregation must accept some responsibility in the work and worship of the church. What each one does will depend upon his ability and other factors, but each individual ought to feel a sense of responsibility toward the work and worship of the church to which he belongs. Regular attendance at the services, cooperation in its work, and earnest prayer for the church is not an unreasonable request to make of the applicant for church membership.

The minister should explain and interpret the yearly cycle of seasons, special days, and other activities of the local church program so that the new member will understand the purpose and have a comprehensive view of these matters. When members see the total program and its parts in relationship to the goals toward which the group is working, they will give better cooperation and special days will have more meaning. Discussing these matters with the members of the congregation is time well spent.

If the local church is to serve its community in providing a place of worship where people will hear the word of God proclaimed and receive the personal ministry of a pastor, money is needed for buildings, salaries and supplies. This money must come from the members of the congregation. The pastor should explain the local financial plan to the applicant and discuss with him the importance of giving regularly and faithfully to the church.

Our money is a part of our life, energy, talent and time that have been exchanged for money. When we give our money to the church, we are giving a part of ourselves to God in a form that can be used to carry on the work of Christian preaching, teaching and healing through the agencies of the church. Through contributions to missions and benevolent interests we share in the work carried on by the denomination and by interdenominational organizations over the world. In this way, one can have a share in doing things that one could never possibly do alone. Our money can go into palces which we could never enter and do things we could never do in person.

It is proper that one of the questions asked of the applicant to church membership should be concerning his willingness to give financial support to the church. The new member should be supplied with offering envelopes. It is well to make this a part of the public act of joining the church by giving the applicant a package of envelopes following his affirmative answer to the question regarding financial support for the church. If the church does not use the offering envelope system, whatever system is used should be fully explained.

The ritual provided by one's own denomination should be faithfully followed in receiving people into the membership of the local church. Proper arrangements should be made with the applicants before hand, and the minister should see to it that all requirements for membership have been met according to the regulations of his church. The people to be received into membership should understand when they are to come forward and what they are to do.

The minister may arrange to receive new members into the church at any public service that is convenient for the

The Reception of Church Members

people and suitable to him. It may come either before or after the sermon. When the time designated for the reception of members has arrived, the pastor should so indicate.

During the prayer, it is impressive to have the applicants kneel and the minister should kneel with them. He should take the hand of each as they are welcomed into the church fellowship. The members of the congregation should be asked to stand when giving their pledge to receive, assist and counsel the new members. If arrangements can be made to have church membership certificates properly made out beforehand, it is well to give these to the new members while they are at the front of the sanctuary.

The ritual should be read reverently and distinctly so all can hear. It should not be hurried. Let the people know that such moments are sacred. It is a holy act of worship when the congregation receives new members, for it is an act of confession and a reaffirmation of faith in which God is glorified.

Chapter 12

HOLY MATRIMONY

MARRIAGE is God's plan for human life. It was so from the very beginning. "And he answered and said, Have ye not read, that he who made them from the beginning made them male and female, and said, For this cause shall a man leave his father and mother, and shall cleave to his wife; and the two shall become one flesh? So that they are no more two, but one flesh. What therefore God hath joined together, let not man put asunder." [1]

The family is the basic unit of society. Life is carried on from one generation to another as a result of the sexual union of a man and a woman. God has ordained that such union shall take place only within the marriage relationship which protects it and hallows it with a spiritual union of mutual love, respect, comradeship and devotion.

One receives his name through the family into which he has been born and he is known first of all as the child of his parents. One's first contact with others is in the home and the experiences there prepare him for living in the community.

The long period of infancy and childhood associated with human life makes the home a very important institution in society, so it is to be expected that there will be civil marriage laws and regulations. The minister and the individuals seeking marriage must know what these regulations are.

---

[1] Matthew 19: 4, 5, 6.

Marriage is also the concern of the Church as well as of society, for it is God's provision for continuing human existence through the birth of new life. It is divinely ordained as that relationship which offers a man and a woman the possibilities of experiencing the highest fulfillment of earthly comradeship.[2]

The marriage ceremony of the Church incorporates the ideals and principles of a Christian home. The minister should interpret these to the couple in a private interview before the day of the wedding. All plans for the wedding should be thoroughly discussed beforehand so that there will be no misunderstanding about the details which vary so greatly according to the customs of the community and the desires of the couple being married. The minister should counsel the couple as needed so that the final plans for the ceremony will include all of the desirable and essential features for an impressive service, and avoid anything that might make it less reverent or less meaningful. Everything that is done should fit into the purpose and spirit of the ceremony.

In the interview with the couple, the minister should give guidance for establishing a Christian home and explain to the couple how important it is to pray and worship together. They should be reminded that the minister is always their friend, and his counsel should be sought whenever they face difficulties or crises in their lives. The wedding ceremony, both its procedure and significance, should be carefully explained and interpreted.

The ceremony opens by directing the thoughts to marriage as a divine plan blessed of God. This is fittingly done in the address to the people assembled and sets the tone for all that

---

[2] Genesis 2: 18-24.

follows. Because marriage is ordained of God, he should be recognized as the authority whose approval must be obtained and before whom vows are made. Since marriage concerns not only the couple being married but all of society, it is proper that it be so expressed in the address to the assembly of people. A minister may desire to read some Scripture following the address to the people. If so, Matthew 19: 4-6 is appropriate.

The two who are presenting themselves for marriage are to be addressed and charged with keeping the vows they are about to make. If additional Scripture is desired, 1 Corinthians 13: 4-8a is appropriate. It describes the quality of love that must undergird a successful and joyful marriage relationship. Prayer at this point is proper, if so desired, for it is fitting to beseech God's blessings upon what is about to take place.

Both the declaration of intention which the couple are requested to make and the vows they take, must incorporate the essentials of marriage. Love is basic to a happy marriage. Mutual fidelity is essential. Sharing life at all levels and under all circumstances is a part of the privilege and responsibility of marriage. The couple must recognize God as the supreme authority according to whose will the course of life must be charted. All of this is implied in the statements which they affirm and in the vows they take. This should be carefully explained to the couple so that they understand the meaning of their vows.

The ring has been associated with the marriage service for centuries and is the most treasured of life's possessions. Its unbroken circle is a reminder of the pledge to love and to cherish each other "so long as both shall live." It is a symbol of the oneness of the couple in the marriage relationship.

In the pronouncement of union which follows the exchange of marriage vows and the giving of the ring, the minister represents both the Church and society, and speaks with the authority of both. This is the reason the minister must inquire if all requirements have been properly met.

The closing prayer presents the two before God in their new relationship. The wedding that has just taken place is only a promise of what is to be. The success of the marriage will be determined by what takes place in the days and years that follow. The wedding is the initial act of marriage. The marriage itself will be what the couple makes it. They will need divine wisdom and counsel to make this relationship what it ought to be.*

The benediction is the climax of the service. It is the moment in which the husband and wife wait for the blessings of God upon the relationship into which they have just entered. They have pledged themselves to mutual comradeship according to God's plan, and when life is ordered according to the divine will, blessings are assured. The minister has the high and holy privilege of lifting up his hands to bless them in God's name.

Plans for the wedding are best discussed after the minister has interpreted the wedding ritual to the couple. Better plans are made for the service when the couple understands its full meaning, and recognizes that it is a religious service in which

---

* The author's book, *Except the Lord Build the House*, is especially helpful for young married couples in establishing the practice of praying together. It makes an inexpensive and attractive gift which a pastor may hand to the couple after the ceremony. It is a devotional book that gives guidance in the fundamental spiritual relationships of marriage. It is published by the Evangelical Press, Harrisburg, Pa. Price, $1.00 in white gift box.

they mutually pledge themselves to a life-long comradeship that unites them as one.

If there are to be many guests at the wedding, a rehearsal will help each person in the wedding party to become familiar with what he is to do and how he is to do it. Such a rehearsal helps the couple and their attendants to be under less strain during the wedding ceremony and leaves them free to give more attention to the purpose and meaning of the service.

Kneeling for prayer is optional, of course, but it is always very impressive. The ritual should be studied by the minister so that he is familiar with each detail. He ought to read it slowly and reverently. The words should be pronounced distinctly and the sentences read with proper emphasis. There should be dignity but not stiffness in the service.

Since this is a service in which several may take part, there are occasions when unexpected things happen. The minister must keep his poise and properly manage whatever comes. A quiet smile when a flower girl does something wrong will put everyone at ease. Give directions to the people at the altar in a low quiet voice when necessary. They are not likely to remember everything they are to do. Do not depend too much upon signals. They may confuse. If the minister is calm and knows just what he wants to do, everyone will be more at ease. The minister should give proper direction at all times.

Music for church weddings ought to be religious in thought and spirit. The minister should give tactful guidance in this matter. He can often suggest appropriate tunes and songs.

One should not permit a photographer to interrupt and detract from the service by taking pictures during the ceremony. The group can pose for pictures afterwards. The wedding is a religious service of worship, too sacred to be treated as a spectacle to be photographed.

When Holy Communion is to be included in the service it should be celebrated between the final prayer and the benediction. The couple should kneel for the prayer and remain kneeling for the sacrament. The celebration of the Lord's Supper should be limited to the essentials—consecration of the elements, words of institution briefly spoken, and the giving of the elements to the couple.

After the benediction by the minister, time should be allowed for the bridal kiss before the recessional march begins. The couple should stand at the altar for the ceremony with the woman at the man's left so that when they march from the altar, the woman is on the man's right.

The details of the wedding service often cause confusion because most of them depend upon the arrangements of the sanctuary and the desires of the couple. Such matters should be given careful attention and the minister should not hesitate to give suggestions. The couple will expect him to counsel them on such matters.

When coming to the altar for the ceremony, the men will use a door at the minister's left if there is one available. If not, they can come down a side isle. Some situations may even require that they come down the center aisle, but the men should not use the central aisle unless there is no other way to reach the altar. The men should take their place at the left of the minister. If there are to be several in the group, the ushers come first, followed by the best man, and finally the groom. Some will want them to come in pairs, others will have each come alone. The physical arrangements of the building as well as personal desires will have to be considered.

In coming to the altar, those in the wedding party must not walk too fast. Many will want them to keep in step with the wedding march. It is important that a rehearsal be held for practice in walking to the altar if there are to be many guests at the wedding.

The women may come in pairs or singly, except of course, the maid of honor should come alone and precede the bride. If there are flower girls and ring bearers, they will follow the maid of honor, preceding the bride. In the formal wedding, the bride will come down the aisle escorted by her father or friend. They will take their place near the altar until the father has given his daughter to be married to the man. He then steps back and the minister will have the group step forward to the altar, with the bride and groom immediately before him. The ceremony will then proceed.

The friends and relatives of the bride sit in the section to the right of the minister as he faces the congregation. The relatives and friends of the groom sit on the left side. The bride's mother is ushered to her place after the groom's mother is seated, and just before the wedding march begins.

The ushers should light the candles at the altar as the organ music begins. They should escort the women guests to their seats. They are also responsible for the seating of all guests. The ushers will see that the white aisle runner is placed for the bride and attend to other details necessary for the proper procedure of the service.

The things that have been written in these last few paragraphs are intended to call attention to some general principles that are to be followed in planning the mechanical details of the wedding ceremony. They will be varied and altered according to the desires of the couple, the number in the wedding party, the formality of the service, the arrangement of the sanctuary, and many other things. The minister will need to counsel the couple in these matters so that the most appropriate things are done to produce the most effective and reverent service.

Chapter 13

THE BURIAL OF THE DEAD

JESUS, on one occasion, stood up in the synagogue and read from Isaiah 61: 1-2—"The Spirit of the Lord God is upon me; because the Lord hath anointed me to preach good tidings unto the meek; he hath sent me to bind up the broken-hearted, to proclaim liberty to the captives, and the opening of the prison to them that are bound; to proclaim the acceptable year of the Lord, and the day of vengeance of our God; to comfort all that mourn." No small part of the minister's task today is to "bind up the broken-hearted" and comfort all that mourn." It is one of the minister's duties to bury the dead.

The funeral service is an occasion for showing respect to the dead and giving comfort to those in mourning. It is not primarily a time for evangelism, but certainly the example of a Christian life and the interpretation of Christian belief about death and the future life ought to be an occasion to arouse a sense of concern in the minds of many who attend the service.

Local custom and the desires of the family will guide the minister in many of the details of the funeral service. He must always keep in mind however, that he is a minister of the gospel, commissioned to do the work of Christ and show forth the compassion of our Lord.

Where only Scripture and prayers are required, the minister can simply follow the ritual of his church. If a sermon is expected, it should follow the reading of Scripture and prayer or a hymn. Some times the minister may be requested to read the hymns instead of having them sung.

In the address, the minister will find it a good policy to major on an exposition of the Christian faith and give comfort to those who mourn rather than spend the time in eulogizing the dead. There are times when eulogy may be appropriate but that is not the chief purpose of a funeral service. It is a service in which we acknowledge the worth of human life by a reverent burial. It provides an occasion for witnessing to the Christian faith as it touches life at the point of death. An exposition of this faith will be a source of comfort to those who mourn and will be profitable instruction to those who are not of the Christian faith.

The entire service should be conducted reverently. It ought not to be of great length but the minister should never give the impression that he is hurried. The length of the service will depend upon the custom of the local community, the desires of the family and the place where the service is held. The minister must exercise his best judgment in these matters.

The minister in charge should constantly keep his chief task in mind. It is to comfort those who mourn and to heal the broken hearted. He must cultivate a spiritual sensitiveness for such occasions, for only in this way can he be most helpful and say what is most appropriate. There are not enough rules to cover every situation. The minister must seek the guidance of God in these matters and he will miss this guidance unless he cultivates a sincere concern for people in their sufferings.

Just as it is through the vicarious suffering of Christ that we have redemption from sin, so the minister will bring redemption and comfort to the sorrowing only as he learns to enter into sufferings which are not his and take upon himself the burdens of others. This is not easy. Redemptive work is always costly. A minister who boasts that a funeral service is easy, gives evidence that he only performs a meaningless ritual of empty words. A funeral ought not to be an empty thing. To enter into the sufferings of others and speak words of comfort to them for the healing of their sorrows requires a personal sharing of one's faith. Like Christ in the healing of the woman who touched his garment, one will be aware that something has gone out of him.[1]

Death often shatters hopes; they must be restored. The darkness of despair must be scattered by the light of new vision. Weakened faith must be strenghtened. Foundations associated with living have been removed; they must be replaced. Hearts that have been chilled by death must be warmed by the Spirit of Life. These things can take place only as the minister completely gives himself at the altar of Christian service. This must include his heart and mind. He must try to feel what they feel, enter into their sorrow, comfort them by sharing his faith with them.

If the minister is to be helpful in time of death, he must pray regularly for his people. This brings him in touch with divine resources. Only as he makes the program of his parish ministry to center in an effort to shepherd individuals according to their needs will he be able to know life's deepest sorrows and speak words of comfort at times of death. The minister must live for those he serves. He must get into their hearts as well as into their homes.

In the long range view, the effectiveness of a man's ministry in hours of death or other crisis periods depends largely

---

[1] Mark 5: 30.

upon what he is in his relationship to Christ and to others. Those who mourn may not remember all of the words the preacher uses at the funeral but they will find comfort in the spirit and faith that he demonstrates and in what they have known him to be in other days. That is why the bereaved often request a certain minister for the funeral service of a loved one. The comforting ministry of a pastor is largely dependent upon the quality of his soul and the personal ministry he has rendered to people on other occasions.

The people of the congregation should be taught to notify the minister as soon as a death occurs, so that he can call upon the family. This does not make him dependent upon a chance hearing of it several hours later. As soon as the minister is told of the death, he should call upon the family. The purpose of the call is to bring comfort to the bereaved and pray with them. At a later call, probably the next day, arrangements for the funeral service can be made.

Chapter 14

ORDINATION

ORDINATION is a high and holy act in which the Church officially sets a man apart for the sacred work of the Christian ministry in recognition of the response which that individual has made to the divine call. A man does not ordain himself. God has called him and the Church authoritatively ordains him a minister of the gospel.

Just as a man feels the hand of God laid upon him in the call to the ministry, so the hands of those in authority in the Church are laid upon his head to set him apart for the task. He thus takes his place in the long line of prophets who have ministered in God's name through the centuries. The service in which this takes place ought to be dignified and reverent. It should follow the ritual of the Church in which is preserved the heritage and spiritual succession of the ministry.

The office of the Christian ministry has been established by God, not through any special word of institution but in the very act of redemption which lies at the center of his dealings with man. The Christian ministry is the continuation and extension of God's reconciling work. Through the ministry of the Word and sacraments, God's redemptive love and power reaches out to sinful men.

Just as redemption is central in the Christian faith so the ministry of redemption is central in the Church. The minister holds a key position in the life and work of the Church. Those who carry on this ministry stand in line with Christ through whom redemption is made possible and through whom they are commissioned to preach the Word and administer the sacraments as means of divine grace.

The office of the ministry is given to the Church by God through Jesus Christ and it is sustained by the Holy Spirit continuing to call men to this place of service. But the ministry is something more than a personal thing between God and the individual. It is also a concern of the Church. The Church must set up standards to test what the candidate interprets as a call to the ministry. The test must be according to those requirements that make for an effective ministry. When the minister is ordained through the ritual of the Church, however, he goes forth with the authority of God. God ordains a man through the Church to be a messenger of redemption.

The minister is a very important person in the life of the Church. He is an administrator, pastor, preacher. He is the voice of God to his generation. He celebrates the sacraments and leads in worship. He is an interpreter of God to men. He is an announcer of redemption, proclaiming the ways of salvation.

The work of the ministry consists of preaching the Word and administering the sacraments as means of grace through which sinful man is reconciled to God. It is rooted in the priestly work of Christ in which he offered himself as a sacrifice on behalf of man. He is the perfect sacrifice, offered once for all.

The work of the ministry is not, therefore, that of a priest offering a sacrifice on behalf of his people as an effort to gain forgiveness from sin, but that of announcing and proclaiming the sacrifice made in Christ. The special priestly office was abolished by Christ and all believers are now priests in the sense of having free access to God. We need no other mediator than Christ. Ordination to the ministry bestows no special religious qualifications upon a man but charges him with special responsibilities in the office of the ministry. There is no basic personal difference between the layman and minister. The difference is in the office. All Christians are obligated to serve God, but not all are commissioned to serve in the office of the ministry.

In Christ the Word of God became flesh. The message God had to give to man was incarnated in a human life. So the minister personalizes the divine message of redemption. He is an intepreter of God and of God's message to men. This is the reason he is often referred to with the word "Reverend," which is a term of respect for the office he represents, not a personal title.

The ordination service is a most holy one. The ritual provided by the denomination to which one belongs should be closely followed. This ritual conforms to the doctrine of the Church and contains those elements essential for a proper ordination to the ministry. The service should be unhurried and reverently carried out according to the prescribed ritual.

Chapter 15

DEDICATIONS AND INSTALLATIONS

BOTH buildings and organizations are important to the worship, fellowship and work of the Church. Dedications of buildings and installations of officials, therefore, have a place in Christian worship. Such dedications and installations ought to reflect Christian thinking in relation to these matters.

The dedication of church buildings is a custom of long standing. Buildings are not needed for God to dwell in but appropriate buildings provide facilities that help us in our worship of him who "dwelleth not in temples made with hands." It is therefore proper that sanctuaries built for worship should be set apart for such use through a service of dedication. It is just as appropriate that buildings erected for the teaching of Christian faith be dedicated to God, for they serve a holy purpose. Hospitals that provide for a ministry of healing and homes which provide needed shelter ought to be set apart in a dedication service.

Services of dedication should be carefully planned and proper arrangements made before the day of dedication. Ground breaking and cornerstone laying services naturally belong out-of-doors. When the weather is bad, the sermon and other parts of the service can be held indoors, so that only the litany and prayers directly associated with the actual ground breaking or cornerstone laying need be used outside.

Various parts of the dedication service can be assigned to the different ministers who may be present. All parts in which the congregation participate should be printed and distributed to all present. In many instances the entire ritual of dedication can be printed and distributed. Where congregational participation is confined to the repetition of the same phrase, that can be so explained and no printed ritual would be required in such instances.

For note burning services it is better to use a facsimile of the note so the original one can be properly preserved and recorded.

Installation services are appropriate because they focus the thought of the congregation and the individuals holding office upon the responsibilities which they carry and the support which those who selected them should give. It is also a reminder that although members have different abilities and different responsibilities, all have a place in the work of the Church. All are parts of the same Body of Christ and our varied abilities are gifts of the Holy Spirit.

Those being installed should be properly instructed in what they are to say. They should likewise be properly instructed concerning their responsibilities in the offices to which they have been elected in the local church.

The spirit of the installation service should be one of mutual consecration in which the officials are properly set apart for their tasks and the congregation dedicates itself to consecrated support and cooperation. An installation service must be a dedication of life to serve Christ in the special task accepted. "Have this mind in you, which was also in Christ Jesus: who, existing in the form of God, counted not the being on an equality with God a thing to be grasped, but emptied himself, taking the form of a servant, being made in the likeness of men; and being found in fashion as a man, he humbled himself, becoming obedient even unto death, yea, the death of the cross."[1]

The details of the installation service will be largely determined by local custom, by the nature of the organization whose officers are being installed, by the nature of the service in which the installation takes place, and by the will of the minister in charge. The installation may come before or after the sermon, depending upon the occasion and the message.

The officers or teachers to be installed are generally called to the chancel, although an effective service can be conducted by having them to stand where they are in the congregation, reminding the people that these officers which have been chosen are fellow Christians assigned specific tasks. When the officers are called to the front, it is very effective to have them kneel for the prayer of consecration after having answered the questions provided in the ritual.

---

[1] Philippians 2: 5-8.